THE LIST
GLASGOW AND EDINBURGH EVENTS GUIDE

contributors

Editor
Willy Maley

Deputy Editor
Brian Donaldson

Writers
Tim Abrahams, Alan Bissett, Bella Bathurst, Christopher Brookmyre, Nick Brooks, Aly Burt, Ron Butlin, Philippa Cochrane, Stuart Cosgrove, Paul Cuddihy, Paul Dale, Des Dillon, Chris Dolan, Anne Donovan, Bill Duncan, Gordon Eldrett, Margaret Elphinstone, Rodger Evans, Jonathan Falla, Miles Fielder, Rodge Glass, Katie Gould, Gerry Hassan, Ruth Hedges, Brian Hennigan, Laura Hird, Kenny Hodgart, Robin Hodge, Nick Holdstock, Richard Holloway, Doug Johnstone, Aaron Kelly, Stuart Kelly, AL Kennedy, Marc Lambert, Jo MacDonald, Katy McAulay, Kevin MacNeil, Laura Marney, Dave Martin, Anna Millar, Denise Mina, Will Napier, Niall O'Gallagher, Andrew O'Hagan, Colette Paul, Allan Radcliffe, Ian Rankin, Johnny Regan, Jay Richardson, James Robertson, Suhayl Saadi, James Smart, Alexander McCall Smith, Ali Smith, Donald Smith, Zoë Strachan, Rachael Street, Louise Welsh

Design & Art Direction
Krista Kegel-Dixon

Promotion
Sheri Friers

Production
Simon Armin, Lucy Reeves

Subeditor
Ashley Davies

Picture Research
Miles Fielder

Publisher
Robin Hodge

Published by The List Ltd
HEAD OFFICE:
14 High Street
Edinburgh EH1 1TE
Tel: 0131 550 3050
Fax: 0131 557 8500
www.list.co.uk
email books@list.co.uk

The publisher acknowledges subsidy from the Scottish Arts Council towards publication of this volume.

ISBN: 1-901077-17-9

www.list.co.uk

Contents

D0279086

sponsored by

orange™

Scottish Arts Council

A&B
Arts & Business Scotland

Scottish **Book** Trust

Introduction

This selection sets out to celebrate the depth and diversity of Scottish literary culture, and testify to the spark and spirit of Scottish prose over four, going on five, centuries. It's a list that states the obvious as well as the obscure, that looks to the living as well as the dead, the popular as well as the privileged, that commits to the contemporary as much as the classical, and that takes the reader from Sir Walter Scott to Irvine Welsh, from Sir Arthur Conan Doyle to Ian Rankin, from *Jekyll and Hyde* to JK Rowling, from the Highland Clearances to the Slum Clearances, and from Trocchi to *Trainspotting*. Split personalities loom large, from *Confessions of a Justified Sinner* to *The Divided Self*. It attempts to balance gender and genre, coverage and quality, canonical status and quirkiness.

This broad church, from *The Bible* to *Buddha Da*, bears witness to the range and richness of Scottish writing. At one end of the period covered we find the *King James Bible*, at the other end is Anne Donovan's acclaimed debut novel which celebrates, in sparkling Scots, a multi-faith and multicultural Scotland much more diverse than that of James. Although a lengthy period in Scottish writing is covered, the ultimate bias is towards recent works: towards the living. The last 15 years in particular have witnessed an unprecedented flowering, and this period is marked by a bevy of books from the 'Nifty Nineties' and the 'Naughty Noughties'.

The compiler of any list of Best Scottish Books is on a *Jekyll and Hyde*-ing to nothing, because they'll never please all sides of the Scottish psyche. Even though they're both as hard as nails, Muriel Spark and Irvine Welsh don't share the same fanbase. This list sets out not to court controversy, but to inspire by celebrating the familiar, unearthing forgotten masterpieces, highlighting the strength of new writing and by bringing together the multiple strands of Scottish literature.

The selection evolved and devolved over months of consideration and debate. At least two professors of Scottish literature weighed in with their opinions, as did several other scholarly experts in Scottish writing, and their contributions were supplemented by those of the reviewers, many of whom are themselves represented on the list. The sheer number of books clamouring for inclusion meant that as well as a top 100, we have included a second 100 of books bubbling under and breaking through.

To make the selection, some guidelines had to be established and early on we decided to take 'book' to mean a published work consisting of a single narrative or thesis. Thus it embraces works of continuous prose, chiefly novels, but also some major non-fiction works of immense philosophical, political and scientific importance. Works of poetry, short stories or drama are not included as we decided it is better to celebrate them on their own terms. We hope to draw up further lists in the future but we have included an appendix giving an overview of the major poets of the stature of Burns, Byron and Morgan and playwrights of the calibre of Barrie, Bridie and Byrne.

Crucially, the list has only one book per author, which made for some hard and hotly debated choices. For example, we had to choose between the enduring popular appeal of Robert Louis Stevenson's *Kidnapped* and the international literary impact and entrenchment in the national psyche of *The Strange Case of Dr Jekyll and Mr Hyde*, between James Kelman's Booker Prize-winning novel *How Late it Was, How Late* and *A Disaffection*, the contemporary classic that propelled him into the front rank of world writers, between the explosive postmodern energy of Alasdair Gray's *Poor Things* and his breathtaking breakthrough book *Lanark*, which transformed the literary representation of Glasgow, making the whole globe appear too small to contain that city's imagination.

It could be objected that this is a list of 100 books by different authors, rather than the best 100 (which might have included most of Galloway, Gray, Kelman, Spark and Stevenson). But some writers are more than authors, they're monuments. Sir Walter Scott could have had half a dozen works in the top 100, but we want to show as many sides to Scotland as possible, and to showcase the forms and genres in which Scotland excels. Which is why we included as much children's fiction, crime writing, fantasy, gothic and historical romance as we could. The adaptability of Scottish writing is illustrated through the inclusion of numerous novels made into films. Gordon Williams' *The Siege of Trencher's Farm*, adapted by Sam Peckinpah as *Straw Dogs*, is one of the most notorious examples, while David Benedictus' novelisation of Bill Forsyth's *Local Hero* is an instance of the process in reverse.

The question of how to define 'Scottish' is always contentious. Our Scotland is a big country and we have opted for as inclusive, elastic and open-minded an approach as possible. You don't need a Scottish passport to gain entry. There are some surprises in store, both in terms of omissions and inclusions. Many of the texts listed here are events as well as publications. Some are out of print, some are out of order and some are out of this world, but all are out of Scotland. Yes, there are must-have works by the major Scottish writers, but there are also mighty tomes by non-Scottish writers published in, written in or set in Scotland.

The inclusion of Woolf, Orwell and Conrad may surprise initially. Woolf saw herself as an 'outsider', and famously remarked 'as a woman, I have no country. As a woman I want no country. As a woman my country is the whole world'. The familiar line on *To the Lighthouse* is that Skye is really St Ives and the Hebrides is really Cornwall, but the book's Scottish connections run deep. In the novel, Mrs Ramsay thinks: 'Still, if every door in a house is left perpetually open, and no lockmaker in the whole of Scotland can mend a bolt, things must spoil. Every door was left open.' This list is an open door, not one locked to outsiders. Since Woolf set her best novel on Skye, we must give her a room of her own in our hotel world.

From Alasdair Gray's Lanark

As for *Nineteen Eighty-Four*, where better to write about Airstrip One and Big Brother than on the west coast of Scotland, future home of the nuclear submarine? Not content to use it for sheep and sport, Big Bro needed a military base. Orwell went to Jura in 1946, staying at Barnhill Farm at the most inaccessible end of the island, an ironic escape from the glare of publicity that followed the publication of *Animal Farm*. The Paps of Jura, its famous peaks, nurtured Orwell's novel. Its original title – *The Last Man in Europe* – chimes with the remoteness of the room where he wrote it.

Conrad's *Heart of Darkness* was first published in Scotland, in three instalments in *Blackwood's Magazine* in February, March and April 1899. Writing to its editor, William Blackwood, Conrad described the magazine as 'the only monthly I care to read', and when he sent the final manuscript to Edinburgh for publication he expressed his profound gratitude. This book – arguably the most distinctive novella in the English language – illustrates the daring and foresight of Scottish publishing. Scotland, the land of Livingstone, embraced Africa, so it's no surprise that Conrad's novel was ushered into being in the World City of Literature.

Many hands make lists work, and this one is no exception. Thanks be to Alan Bissett, Brian Donaldson, Marc Lambert, Dorothy McMillan, Niall O'Gallagher, Murray Pittock, Alan Riach and Robin Hodge, for looking at the list, keeping a straight face and saving me from gracelessness. All errors and oversights are mine alone. Maley culpa.

From Alan Spence's *The Magic Flute* to Jackie Kay's *Trumpet*, this list blows loud and long for Scottish literature, celebrating an unparalleled body of work. So here are 100 books of Scotitude, with attitude. If the future's bright, then the past is brilliant, judging by the variety and vibrancy of the books brought to light here. From Scott to Welsh, here are a hundred blooming thistles, some jaggy nettles and some bonny blooming heather. In days of yore, to 'enter the lists' meant to pass through the palisades enclosing a tilt-yard, the scene of a jousting contest. Nowadays, to 'enter the lists' means to issue a challenge, or accept one. The challenge here was to put together a list of Scottish books that does justice to the breadth and brio of Scottish writing. It is up to the reader to pick up the gauntlet.

In the end, finding the best book in Scotland will be a public choice, not a personal one. It cannot be decided by committee, only by community, and after the widest possible consultation. The winner of the Best Scottish Book will be chosen over the coming months by you, the readers, and announced at the Edinburgh International Book Festival this August.

Professor Willy Maley
School of English and Scottish Language and Literature,
University of Glasgow
March 2005

Vote for your favourite book…

Text the word 'VOTE' and the name of your favourite Scottish book to 81800. Your name will automatically go into a prize draw to win one of the fabulous prizes we are giving away including books, mobile phones & talk time plus a grand prize of a trip to an international book festival abroad.

100 Best Scottish Books
of all time

Adam Blair
JG Lockhart (1822)

In a society where church scandals are nothing new, it is hard to imagine the tale of a minister committing adultery causing a great uproar. But in 1822, JG Lockhart's novel was heavily criticised for its portrayal of a widowed minister who has an affair with a married woman.

The protagonist Adam Blair is a model churchman, but after the death of his wife he suffers from great loneliness and a dearth of like-minded company, since the simple, rural community in which he lives provides little in the way of intellectual stimulation. However, the unexpected arrival of his wife's cousin Charlotte Campbell fills this gap, as the pair debate spiritual matters and share the care of Blair's only child Sarah. While tongues wag among his friends in the city about the relationship, the parishioners and Blair himself continue to believe that a man of his position is above falling. Such is their innocence that when the minister does eventually succumb to his passion for Charlotte, it is a sin for which he cannot forgive himself.

Immoral is not the only charge that has been levelled at Lockhart's novel as some critics have slammed the plot and characters for being rather flimsy. Yet, the rich descriptions of nature provide a powerful subtext and mirror the eponymous character's repressed emotions. *Adam Blair* was based on the true story of a local minister who was deposed in 1746, but went on to marry his mistress and was eventually accepted back into the church. But Lockhart does not allow such an easy ending and includes a stern warning. 'I have told a *true story*. I hope the days are yet far distant when it shall be doubted in Scotland that such things might have been.' (Rachael Street)

Annals of the Parish
See panel, page 7.

An Oidhche Mus Do Sheòl Sinn
Aonghas Pàdraig Caimbeul (2003)

The title of Aonghas Pàdraig's first full-length novel means 'The Night Before We Sailed'. Few novels have been published in Scottish Gaelic and many of those that have are aimed at children and school pupils. This makes the author's achievement in this ambitious and outward looking novel even more startling. It is thrilling to experience a book like this in Gaelic. *An Oidhche Mus Do Sheòl Sinn* is a joy to read, moving and beautifully written.

The novel was shortlisted for the Saltire Book of the Year Award in 2004 and came second in that year's BBC's *Taghadh nan Leabhar*, in which the audience voted for their favourite Gaelic book. It follows the lives of a South Uist family separated by war, geography and political commitment through the 20th century. Alasdair is decorated for his service during World War

Sunshine by Robert Thorburn Ross,
The National Gallery of Scotland

Annals of the Parish
John Galt (1821)
Reviewer: Andrew O'Hagan

John Galt was born in Irvine, made his name in London, money in Canada, and died and was buried in Greenock in 1839. He was Coleridge's favourite novelist and a star contributor to *Blackwood's Magazine*. In the 1820s, he wrote a series of Scots stories, or 'theoretical histories' as he called them, his 'Tales of the West', the greatest of which is his novel *Annals of the Parish*. In many ways, it is the miniature masterpiece of small-town Scottish life, a portrait of human character and social change more particular and more beautifully coloured than anything by Walter Scott. Reading it, you begin to imagine that Flemish painting found its Scottish counterpart in a writer of fiction: the book is full of human things and natural oddities, while the humour is very gentle and the language exact.

The book is narrated by the Reverend Micah Balwhidder, a Presbyterian minister in the Ayrshire town of Dalmailing, and covers the years 1760 to 1810, the period of Robert Burns and the Industrial Revolution, when the economic and moral shape of Scottish life was changing in ways both explicit and invisible. The novel charts all this: the work of smugglers at Troon, new births in the parish, old deaths, the efforts of the press-gangs, the rise of the local economy, the business of 'cadgers by day and excisemen by night', the opening of a new dance school at Irville, 'run by Mr Macskipnish', visits to Glasgow and Edinburgh, the day of the country fair,

described with a rare vernacular beauty. It's a precursor to Dickens in terms of detail and to Flaubert in terms of style.

Galt was interested in small incidents and he understood, in a very modern way, how a Scottish novel could work by accretion: social detail, human voices and psychological inflection working together to raise reality. He created several works of art this way, but *Annals of the Parish* is singular mainly, I think, because of the way Balwhidder's narrative voice works. He is hungry for the milk of human kindness, yet also he is vain and conceited, concerned – perhaps too concerned – with the workings of prosperity. The Reverend Balwhidder contains multitudes, and his distinctive humanity, his small failings, his linguistic rightness, make him as great a fictional hero, to my mind, as Don Quixote or David Copperfield or Leopold Bloom.

Further reading: *Sir Andrew Wylie* (1820) is a grand historical epic, and arguably one of the first murder mysteries; *The Radical* (1832) traces the campaign for parliamentary reform.

Andrew O'Hagan
is the author of The Missing, Our Fathers, *and* Personality.

PHOTO: JERRY BAUER

Courtesy of Canongate Books

Born Free
Laura Hird (1999)
Reviewer: Kevin MacNeil

Laura Hird's *Born Free* is a masterpiece of contemporary urban fiction. It is also a quintessentially Scottish book: funny but dark, malevolent but life affirming, poignant but endearingly compulsive. First published in 1999, *Born Free* followed Hird's *Nail and Other Stories*, a collection which, through its vivid characterisation, black humour and energetic use of language, immediately marked Hird as a talent to look out for.

She initially appeared in the semi-legendary *Rebel Inc* magazine, which gave rise to the Canongate imprint that first published her books. This was also the background from which talents such as Irvine Welsh and Alan Warner emerged. Hird is the only great female writer of that group and she has been, I feel, somewhat underrated. *Born Free* is a classic, pure and simple. It tells the story – from different points of view – of one very Scottish, very urban, very dysfunctional working-class family. Vic is a bored bus driver whose best just doesn't seem to be good enough. Angie is his cheating, alcoholic wife. Joni is their 15-year-old daughter, desperate to lose her virginity, and Jake their bullied, tormented 13-year-old son.

Each chapter is told from the point of view of a different member of the family. It's a tough narrative trick to pull off but Hird manages each distinctive voice with a brilliant understanding of what motivates people of different ages and genders to act as they do. She explores her characters' worlds like the compassionate director of an appallingly gripping docu-drama, homing in on themes such as alcoholism, infidelity, working-class lack

of freedom, familial claustrophobia and the yearnings, frustrations and epiphanies of teenage and mid-life crises. Hird shows us there is fundamentally no difference between the ordinary and the extraordinary. It is a virtuoso performance.

Although Hird owes some measure of influence to her peers, a closer scrutiny of her work reveals the influence of Patricia Highsmith and Ian McEwan; *Born Free* is a very filmable novel, though it would be closer to Mike Leigh's work than that of the *Trainspotting* team. Nominated for the Orange Prize, shortlisted for the Whitbread First Novel of the Year and voted *The Face*'s top book of 1999, it was a critical and commercial success. However, I would like to have seen it achieve, on its own terms, what *Trainspotting* did. Perhaps the follow-up, which Hird is currently planning, will accomplish all that and more.

Further reading: *Nail and Other Stories* (1997) is the first collection of Hird's tough, blackly funny short stories, also showcased in the anthology *Children of Albion Rovers* (1996).

Kevin MacNeil *is the author of Love & Zen in the Outer Hebrides, Less Is More Or Less More, and Be Wise Be Otherwise. His new book, The Stornoway Way, is published in August 2005.*

PHOTO: WEK ANDERSON

I and settles in England where he has no contact with his family until one of his sisters arrives on his doorstep. Màiri rides south to join the International Brigade and fight against fascism in the Spanish Civil War. Eòin's vocation to the priesthood takes him first to Aberdeen and then to Spain before bringing him back to Uist where he must re-examine what he has learned in the light of growing uncertainty.

The novel is itself an act of piety. Its broad scope connects the present to the past, the Islands to Europe and the wider world. Its language is rich with the Gaelic of Uist, with new words and old stories, with the knowledge that inventiveness might be the best service one can do to any tradition. Gaelic fiction in the 21st century could not have got off to a better start. (Jo MacDonald/Niall O'Gallagher)

Behind the Scenes at the Museum
Kate Atkinson (1995)

How many books have you read recently that begin with 25 pages conducted, quite amicably, from inside the womb? This one, told in part through the eyes of unwanted baby Ruby Lennox (conception onwards), and in part through the tragic history of her family, is like two great novels in one, opening with surely one of the best first sentences ever: 'I exist!'

Whether documenting a soldier crossing a battlefield to save a dog, or telling us Ruby's mother's words on seeing her daughter for the first time – 'Looks like a piece of meat, take it away' – Kate Atkinson's writing is masterfully controlled. Never overstated, never over-dramatic, she doesn't feel the need to explain how shocking events are. Indeed, she specialises in the kind of arm's length delivery that Raymond Carver made his own, and this comes strongly to mind while reading both storylines, which cross decades of family history and the whole of Ruby's life. For example, the horrors of both World Wars are often understood through Ruby's female ancestors, a neat device which allows the reader to see just how little they understand of the brutal realities, but also how reluctant the men are to tell them about it. This contrasts perfectly with the naive, upbeat delivery of Ruby's child voice.

Behind the Scenes at the Museum is weighted perfectly, changing between its two main strands at just the right moment and entertaining at all points in between. When, on Coronation Day, a two-year-old Ruby looks outside to see her father humping against a wall someone who is definitely not her mother, the magic is in a childish preoccupation with her lost tricycle. This mature debut will surely inspire decades from now, and shows how powerful fiction can be in making us understand real life. (Rodge Glass)

Black and Blue
Ian Rankin (1997)

Ian Rankin is one of this country's most prolific and commercially successful authors. No writer has chronicled the changing face of Edinburgh so vividly nor in such minute detail. Since 1987's *Knots and Crosses*, the investigations of his celebrated creation John Rebus have taken the former SAS operative turned hard-drinking detective and pop music aficionado right across the capital, from tourist spot to seedy underbelly.

So, why single out *Black and Blue* for particular praise? Firstly, the Golden Dagger Award-winning novel finds Rankin really hitting his stride in balancing various plot strands and diversions. The book opens with the brutal death of a North Sea oil worker, which leads Rebus to Aberdeen, the rigs and possible mob connections. The flight north arrives at exactly the right time to avoid some awkward questions concerning a re-opened case, during which Rebus may have been complicit in bending the rules to secure a conviction. Into these threads and among the characteristically gritty, realistic verbal exchanges, Rankin effortlessly weaves a series of copycat killings, aping the pattern of the notorious Bible John who enjoyed a brief reign of fear in Glasgow in the 1960s. Meanwhile the 'Johnny Bible' phenomenon is being observed with uneasy fascination by the original perpetrator.

Rankin's ability to direct these divergent strands towards an exhilarating conclusion is nothing less than astonishing. Also exceptional is the way in which the author applies his talent for brilliantly evoking a place and its history to the wider Scotland, boldly lifting the hard-bitten detective from his usual haunting ground and allowing him to cast his disparaging eye around the ever-changing west and north. (Allan Radcliffe)

Born Free
See panel, page 8.

The Break-Up of Britain: Crisis and Neo-Nationalism
Tom Nairn (1977)

Twenty-five years after Thatcherism and the Falklands, New Labour and Iraq, who can now dispute that the British state is a

strange, untamed beast, unreformed, still not fully at ease in the modern age, and shaped by memory of empire and imperial delusion? If this is now a more widely held view today, it is in part because Tom Nairn's arguments in *The Break-Up of Britain* have been vindicated over time.

The book was first published in 1977 while a second edition appeared in 1981, remaining out of print for 20 years, before a new internet only edition was published in 2003. It's a prescient, historically wide-ranging and polemical tour de force, written in the style and language which Nairn so excels at. It covers everything: the state of Scottish identity, the nature of UKania, but really it is about the role of civic nationalism and identities in a world shaped by powerful economic forces and globalisation. Sometimes Nairn goes over the top, such as his over-pathologising of the Scottish condition, but his words and analysis repay repeated visits time and again.

Sceptics have argued that the *Break-Up* thesis has been invalidated because the United Kingdom is still together all these years later. However, what Nairn shows us is that the present day nature of the country is untenable, and that devolution is too late and too small a change to alter power, culture and identities across these isles. The continuation of the UK in its present form, Nairn believes, is at a cost to all of us within it, and the wider world. Given the Blairite liberal imperialist project – which has seen the UK involved in Kosovo, Sierra Leone, Afghanistan and Iraq – has contributed to global instability and created the conditions for more terrorism, rather than less, perhaps the UK should carry a health warning. (Gerry Hassan)

Brond
Frederic Lindsay (1984)

A political thriller, but a cut above the disposable airport novels of Tom Clancy, *Brond* throws a serpentine plot of political intrigue into central Scotland. After witnessing the mysterious Brond kill a child in Kelvingrove Park, student Robert is drawn into his Machiavellian plan to trap a dangerous IRA killer in hiding on the British mainland. Throw in a Scottish nationalist terrorist cell, an adolescent protagonist on the verge of manhood and the obligatory love interest and *Brond* becomes a Glaswegian *Day of the Jackal*. And so much more.

Ex-teacher Lindsay raises his work to the next level by weaving the action and drama into a wider tapestry, injecting percipient insights and questions about responsibility

and nationhood into a high-octane page-turner that transcends its hokey premise. That he does so without recourse to literary pyrotechnics or any great innovation led to the book suffering in comparison with other Scottish works upon its 1984 release; none too great a slight when James Kelman's *The Busconductor Hines* or Alasdair Gray's *1982, Janine* debuted in the same year. Nonetheless, Lindsay proved himself a formidable author, writing in a disreputable genre by making the familiar strange, twisting well known streets into a landscape of danger and unpredictability at odds with what we think we know.

Brond was later adapted into a three-part series for Channel 4, helmed by Broxburn-born director Michael Caton-Jones, most memorable for giving John Hannah his first starring role and for its oddly operatic soundtrack courtesy of Bill Nelson of Be-Bop Deluxe. Lindsay's *Jill Rips* was then made into a Hollywood movie 'starring' Dolph Lundgren, and the author has since crafted a series of books featuring the Edinburgh detective DI Jim Meldrum, who may not have penetrated the popular consciousness quite like Rankin's Rebus, but continues to keep crime aficionados hooked. (Dave Martin)

Buddha Da
See panel, page 11.

The Bull Calves
Naomi Mitchison (1947)

Naomi Mitchison is one of Scotland's most prolific and impressive 20th century writers, although her work has not received the attention it deserves. She wrote *The Bull Calves* during World War II which she spent mainly at Carradale House in Kintyre and it was a novel that was key to the reinvention of herself as a Scottish writer, after nearly 20 years as part of the London literary scene.

The Bull Calves is a landmark novel, in terms both of Mitchison's career and of Scottish historical fiction. Like Neil Gunn, Mitchison saw the past as a way of highlighting contemporary concerns, and was writing at a time when the Highlands were in economic and cultural decline. Here, she invokes parallels between Scotland in 1947 and 1747, when the novel is set, while drawing on her own family (the Haldanes of Perthshire) and incorporating historical figures into her narrative. In a highly charged atmosphere of uncertainty and distrust, Jacobite sympathisers and political realists struggle to come to terms with the aftermath of the

Courtesy of Burrell Collection

Buddha Da
Anne Donovan (2003)
Reviewer: Paul Cuddihy

From the opening paragraph of *Buddha Da*, there is a lyrical beauty about this book. It reminds me of my favourite songs, the ones that take me somewhere special whenever I hear them. So it is with Anne Donovan's novel. The story of Jimmy, the Glaswegian painter whose decision to become a Buddhist irrevocably changes his family, is told in my own tongue; and the language of Glesga, so often considered rough and uncompromising, has never been made to sound so poetic and smooth. Jimmy's search for spiritual answers could be seen as a mid-life crisis. It affects his apparently happy marriage, with his daughter a sometimes bemused, sometimes astute observer.

Anne Donovan tells the story in three distinct voices: those of Jimmy, his wife Liz and their 12-year-old daughter Anne-Marie. It's a difficult task which is accomplished with apparent ease. It also allows a different experience of the novel whenever it's approached. The first time I read *Buddha Da*, I found Anne-Marie's voice easiest to engage with, Liz's the hardest to relate to and Jimmy's the one that annoyed me the most. 'Pull yourself together, man,' I shouted at the pages. Maybe I empathised more with his wife than I cared to admit? When I read it a second time, it was with a surprising degree of sympathy for Jimmy. Maybe it's just that I'm getting older and should warn my nearest and dearest of impending erratic behaviour, or a sudden quest for some sort of spiritual contentment.

Jimmy's conversion to Buddhism could be a break with the religion of his past, or a way of living for the future. Or maybe it's all just a gamble; Jimmy as the Glasgow Dice Man, throwing a one to become one with oneself. Religion and spirituality is important in the novel, just as it is a part of Glasgow's character. If anyone asked me to name a Catholic Scottish novel, I would cite *Buddha Da*. It's not only because of the background of the McKenna family, whose cradle Catholicism wafts out of every page like Benediction incense despite Jimmy's pursuance of Buddhism, or the trinity of voices that tell the story. It is also in the imminent birth of a baby, as the novel draws to a close, which offers hope for a better future and a possible redemption of Jimmy and Liz's relationship.

I said the book reminded me of my favourite songs and if *Buddha Da* was a record it would be the Smiths' self-titled debut album. I can't say better than that.

Further reading: *Hieroglyphics* (2001) features an array of female voices from innocence to experience in a warmly observed, moving collection of stories.

Paul Cuddihy
*is a short story writer
and editor of
The Celtic View.*

1991 Communicado and
Tramway co-production

The Cone-Gatherers
Robin Jenkins (1955)
Reviewer: Stuart Cosgrove

In what circumstances is kleptomania acceptable; almost certainly when a nation's culture is at stake? It hardly rates as the crime of the century but I once stole a conifer from the floor of the Tramway, after a memorable production of Communicado's *The Cone-Gatherers*. The stage had been scattered with cones and the audience sat amongst autumnal logs watching a piece of Scottish theatrical history unfold. Something impulsive made me want to keep a memento of the performance so, pathetically, I stole one of the props, and now have it hidden away in a drawer like a relic of understanding.

I had read Robin Jenkins' *The Cone-Gatherers* years before, but it was the theatre adaptation that encouraged me to read it again. Sometimes it is on the second or third visitation that you really begin to understand a great book. Superficially, this is a story about the land and the mundane localness of its characters, but at a more metaphoric level it's about renewal, future growth and the capacity of Scotland to rebuild itself.

World War II is still raging in Europe when two brothers arrive at a forest to gather cones so that the seeds can be used to replant trees destroyed by the conflict. The younger brother Calum is a mentally retarded hunchback forced into being a runner for the hunt, racing for his life against a rural landscape at once ugly and spectacular.

Jenkins has not enjoyed any of the attention heaped upon many other Scottish writers and it may be that he's

an acquired taste rather than a minor literary afterthought; but, in an era in which there is renewed interest in Scottish literature he's an author rich in potential.

It would not be too demonstrative to claim that *The Cone-Gatherers* is Scotland's *Cherry Orchard*, a great Chekhovian masterpiece that uses forests and the natural landscape to capture a moment of profound social change. It feels as eerily prescient today as it did when it was first published in the 1950s and is the kind of book that offers up new, modern meanings with every reading. Once you have read the book, it will then seem natural to follow it with Jenkins' other significant work, *A Would-Be Saint*, possibly the only great work of contemporary fiction that alludes to St Johnstone in its title. Or so I desperately like to think.

Further reading: *Fergus Lamont* (1980) traces the life of an illegitimate child from Glasgow's slums; *Childish Things* (2001) focuses on a septuagenarian widower whose carefully suppressed past returns to haunt him when he goes to live with his daughter.

Stuart Cosgrove
is Channel 4's director of nations and regions and the author of Hampden Babylon.

Jacobite Risings and to engage with the future of a ruptured Scotland. Like much of her fiction, the novel examines issues of communality and conflicting loyalties. At the centre is Kirstie Haldane, member of a Whig family, married to Jacobite William Macintosh of Borlum. The richness and warmth of their relationship ensures that the novel, ranging over dark events and deep divisions, ends on a note of optimism.

Mitchison projects into the book her personal experience of life in Kintyre, the impact of war and the loss of her seventh child who survived only one day. She was increasingly concerned with the post-war future of the Highlands, and for many years contributed energetically to Highland politics as well as being a powerful literary voice. (Jenni Calder)

But n Ben A-Go-Go
Matthew Fitt (2000)

Who would have thought that the third millennium would blast off with a sci-fi novel written in Scots? Matthew Fitt's debut leaves granny's hieland hame behind and claims the Scots language for writing that is out of this world. Fitt is one of the people behind Itchy Coo, which publishes Scots language books for children. With *But n Ben A-Go-Go*, Fitt takes the playfulness of his work with bairns into darker territory, writing a work of dystopian fiction that is surely the first of its kind.

But n Ben A-Go-Go is set in the year 2090, half a century since the polar ice caps melted leaving most of Scotland under water. What is left of the population live in a group of floating cities, or parishes, known collectively as Port. A deadly virus called Sangue de Verde has made physical love a thing of the past. Cyberjanny Paolo Broon has watched his infected wife deteriorate, one of many hundreds locked in coffin-like life support machines and kept alive so that the virus will be unable to spread further. As Paolo and Nadia had not even kissed outside cyberspace, his pain is made worse by the knowledge that his wife has been unfaithful. Paolo receives a message from his estranged father and sets off believing that he can lead him to Nadia's cure.

By bringing Scots into contact with this post-apocalyptic future world, Fitt creates a prose that crackles with energy and invention. Like other science fiction writers, he creates a new language to describe this world but his verbal pyrotechnics are even more startling in Scots. *But n Ben A-Go-Go* shows us that

the Scots language can describe worlds as various and exotic as the imaginations of those who use it. (Niall O'Gallagher)

Children of the Dead End
Patrick MacGill (1914)

Patrick MacGill's autobiographical novel roams from the tenant farms of Ireland and the grinding poverty of Dermod Flynn's childhood, to the byways and backroads of Scotland and the navvying life. Leaving home at the age of 12 to seek work 'beyond the hills', Dermod is barely shod and fed, worked to exhaustion by a series of indifferent tenant farmers, and runs away to join the emigrants headed for Scotland in the hope of catching up with his sweetheart Norah Ryan. It is here, tramping between the model lodging houses of Paisley and Glasgow and work at the building of the Kinlochleven Dam that he first encounters Moleskin Joe and Carroty Dan, a man so quick-tempered that upon their first encounter Dermod is forced to thrash him into insensibility.

Taken under the wing of Moleskin, Dermod soon learns the navvies' ways, and were it not for a nascent literary talent, would likely have lived and died on 'the dead end'. An existence of Sisyphean struggle, the life the navvy can expect is nasty, brutish and short. Writing for the London papers presents an exit for Dermod, yet he is uncomfortable among the middle-classes, barely able to use a knife and fork, and still dreams of finding his love Norah somewhere on the Glasgow streets. Tiring of journalism and men who 'played with ideas' Dermod heads once more for Scotland to find Norah. The novel is, therefore, also a moving tale of lost love.

Like his contemporary Jack London, MacGill's early experiences engendered in him a loathing of injustice, and politically radicalised him at a time when British socialism was still in its infancy. Raw, lyrical, angry, *Children of the Dead End* still retains its affecting power.
(Nick Brooks)

The Citadel
AJ Cronin (1937)

In recent years, Jed Mercurio's novel *Bodies* and its subsequent television adaptation have provided shocking insight into the mental and physical strain suffered by overworked medical staff, including consequent fatal lapses in judgement. Rewind some 70 years, and discover AJ Cronin graphically blowing the whistle on the corrupt medical establishment in his sweeping autobiographical novel *The Citadel*.

The girl's name Wendy didn't exist until the publication of JM Barrie's *Peter Pan*. It derived from Barrie's childhood nickname 'friendy-wendy'.

To vote for your favourite Scottish book text the word '**VOTE**' and the name of the book to **81800**

Text charged at your network rate

Ian Rankin's non-writing jobs have included chicken factory worker, alcohol researcher, swineherd, grape picker, tax collector and vocalist in punk band the Dancing Pigs.

The novel's opening segment introduces the protagonist Andrew Manson, a young and idealistic Scottish medical graduate from a lower-class background reporting for duty in his first job. Initially, Manson comes across as an early James Herriot, the fish-out-of-water enthusiast who gradually gains the trust and respect of his patients in a small Welsh mining town with his solicitous methods, eschewing ineffectual medicine for dietary and sanitation improvements. Yet, as the story progresses, Manson's career develops, eventually transferring the doctor and his wife Christine to London where he encounters ingrained corruption on every level of his vocation. Ultimately, Manson's resistance to the baseness of 'the Citadel' (his mocking name for the medical establishment) breaks down, and his professional ethics start to wane in favour of easy money and a comfortable life.

Cronin's novel – particularly the fraught final stages – still has the pace and power to compel. One inhibition for modern readers is that Manson's wife Chris is something of a one-dimensional cipher, a goody-two-shoes schoolteacher whose vain attempt to encourage her husband to follow a virtuous path is contrasted with the lack of honesty Manson encounters from jaded medical practitioners. Conversely, the book's greatest strength is Cronin's unflinching willingness to depict man's fallibility, brilliantly embodied in his hero. (Allan Radcliffe)

A Concussed History of Scotland

Frank Kuppner (1990)

The kind of exercise in post-modernity that makes traditionalists drop their monocles in disbelief at the self-indulgence of it all, *A Concussed History of Scotland* earned Kuppner huge critical acclaim but, perhaps understandably, didn't trouble any bestseller lists. Splitting the fragmented ramblings of an unidentified consciousness into 500 chapters, a maelstrom of name and place, date and time that would have James Joyce blushing at its obtuseness, this novel loves to play with readers' expectations, poking and prodding them into action with a big metaphysical stick.

That it straddles the line between surrealism and the avant garde without ever leaving the reader too detached reveals Kuppner to be an extremely funny writer, although he often hides it well under a blizzard of abrasive aphorisms and sceptical insight underpinned by a vicious intellect which drove him to ask if Scotland

is 'small enough'. And all this in a book that could probably be enjoyed by rolling a dice to decide which chapter to read next without any discernible loss in sense, yet criticised by some as too articulate or for its lack of orientating centre or 'key' to a greater universal truth.

Not particularly Scottish in outlook or language, but still unmistakably of this nation in its preoccupations, Kuppner's career has seen him mining a vein of Scottish fiction vastly different from the bestsellers of Kennedy, Rankin or Welsh. For while he has been compared most often to Alasdair Gray, his work actually stands closest to the Pulitzer-winning prose-poet Charles Simic, whose Yugoslav-American compositions revolve around the impossibility of meaning and empathy and the lack found in all language.

A great Scottish writer then, because he doesn't limit himself to the country's literary tradition, instead demonstrating an intimidating verbal dexterity which draws also on European and Asian influences, Kuppner is this nation's one-man new wave. (Dave Martin)

The Cone-Gatherers

See panel, page 12.

Confessions of an English Opium-Eater

See panel, page 15.

Consider the Lilies

Iain Crichton Smith (1968)

Iain Crichton Smith was, and is, lovingly acknowledged as one of modern Scotland's foremost writers, wits and all-round 'characters'. Generations of readers have grown up holding close to their hearts (and exam cram sheets) one or other of his terse, lyrical poems. There is, however, a great deal more to his oeuvre than his poetry. Reading Iain Crichton Smith – like the author's own compulsion to write – is a hungry addiction. And a blessing.

He was an inconsistent writer – too prolific according to some – penning a staggering number of poems, plays, short stories, essays and novels in both English and Gaelic. He was so humble in his lacerating self-criticisms that some of his critics believed him. He wrote his best known novel *Consider the Lilies* in less than a fortnight; and it is loaded with anachronisms. But who cares that it contains references to postmen, grandfather clocks and footballs when these didn't exist in the Highlands? As ICS pointed out, Shakespeare himself employed

1990 production
(Opium Eaters),
courtesy of BBC

Confessions of an English Opium-Eater

Thomas De Quincey (1822)
Reviewer: Suhayl Saadi

Thomas De Quincey's debut is an intense exploration of the liminal, from the evanescing 'beatific druggist' and the illuminatus prostitute of Oxford Street to the phantasmagoric godfather of logos revolutionaries such as Baudelaire, Kafka, Woolf, Huxley, Borges, Camus, Kerouac, Trocchi and Burroughs. At Oxford, the neuralgic De Quincey turned on, tuned in and dropped out, becoming besotted with Wordsworth, Coleridge et al (though latterly his relationship with the junkie 'mariner' was often tense). He lived much of his adult life (co-habiting with an hallucinatory Nile crocodile) in Edinburgh, working as an essayist, journalist and critic for *Blackwood's* and *London* magazines, and becoming, by degrees, 'The Pope of Opium-Eaters'.

Confessions documents 'the whole of my past life, not as recalled by an act of memory, but as if present and incarnated in the music'. Continually revising the text which, like his own being, he saw as broken, contingent, ambiguous and mediated by both printing press and reader, De Quincey quite simply expanded the concept of prose. Shaman, synaesthetist, syncretist, proto-psychoanalyst, explorer of worlds both abstract and analytic, hawker of paradox, irony and dialectic: De Quincey was integrated by opium.

Even as it punctures utilitarianism, *Confessions* documents the political economy of consciousness. It is an imperialist, Orientalist text — and unlike many of the other Romantics, this Mancunian dope-fiend was always a Reform Conservative — yet there is an intense, struggling integrity and a recognition of context: the authorial subject as object. A visionary creative tension arises from the fugue of revelatory unity and 'a thousand fantastic variations'. An analysis of the effects of mills, microchips and corporatism on the mind seems even more relevant today: 'Might it not be as well to ask after the most beautiful road, rather than the shortest?'

The text is repeatedly 'broken' by digressions and footnotes; the opium-eater as polymath. Surrounded by tomes of German metaphysics, ('I read Kant and again I understood him or fancied that I did') in the depths of a Scottish midwinter, he decanted prodigiously of the ruby-coloured laudanum. It is too easy to adopt the moral high ground. Europe was a bloodbath; De Quincey took opium. The late daguerreotypes betray the face of a broken prophet, someone whose life exists in virtuality, in the text. To read *Confessions* is to read oneself; 'there is no such thing as forgetting', there is no escape. An habitué of the debtors' prison, for De Quincey it was not easy to earn a living as a writer. Nothing changes.

Further reading: *The Knocking at the Gate in Macbeth* (1823) similarly examines altered states; *Murder Considered as One of the Fine Arts* (1827) is an investigation into the criminal mind.

Suhayl Saadi
*is the author of
Psychoraag and
The Burning Mirror.*

PHOTO: BASH KHAN

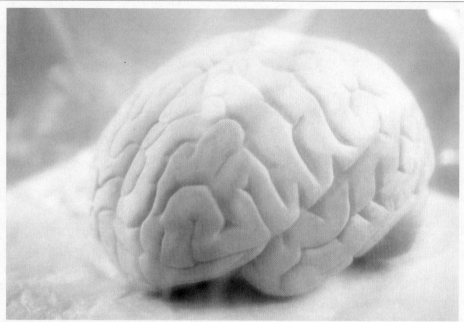

Courtesy of Getty Images

The Divided Self
RD Laing (1960)
Reviewer: Des Dillon

Cometh the hour cometh the book. I had a bit of a Jungian experience with *The Divided Self*. I'd been working on a play in which the main character is schizophrenic and was trawling my bookcases for drama as I like to read a lot of plays when I'm writing. I took out a chunk of Methuen plays with their distinctive blue spines, and among them was *The Divided Self*. I'd never heard of it and didn't know what it was doing in my bookcase. I read the back cover: 'Dr Laing's first purpose is to make madness and the process of going mad comprehensible.' Serendipity of the highest order.

What a delight when I discovered Laing was Glaswegian and the case studies, which proved invaluable, were also Glaswegians. So was my main character. I expected it to focus on clinical psychiatry and be so removed from the human experience of mental illness as to be little use to a writer. But Laing takes an existential approach which is bolstered by actual case studies of patients estranged from themselves and from society. And although requiring intellectual effort at times, this book resonates with humanity. I found it rewarding well beyond the scope of the play I was writing and learned a lot about myself, imagination and humanity.

It came as some relief to me that the schizophrenic I had created, based on a friend of mine, was, by Laing's standards, pretty accurate. But accuracy isn't authenticity.

I used this book to create such authenticity of character that I went beyond what might have been possible without it. I found the explanatory chapters interesting enough but the case studies engulfed me.

I even, at times, began to fear for my own sanity, such was the incisiveness of the prose. One night lying in bed, when my wife was asleep, I held my hand in the air and tried to disassociate from it (such disassociation is one of the early symptoms of schizophrenia). I stared and stared at my hand. When I eventually managed to disassociate I got such a rush of fear coupled with an insight into the schizophrenic's dread. All in all I have been enriched as a human being and had my artistic horizons expanded. I am still writing that play and as I search my character's soul for its deepest and most exalted possibilities, this book, for me, is something of a compass.

Further reading: *Self and Others* (1961) explores the relationship between past experience and current behaviour; *Knots* (1970) is Laing's deceptively simple guide to the ins and outs of human relationships.

Des Dillon
is the author of 11 books, including Me and Ma Gal, Itchycooblue, and Six Black Candles.

anachronisms and who are we to criticise?

It's a novel about the inequitable Highland Clearances, a subject so open-wounded it still angers Gaels today. Yet, contrary to its initial publisher's claims, *Consider the Lilies* is not an historical novel. It's a poet's impassioned meditation on themes of injustice, (anti-)Calvinism, miscommunication and the integral power of frailty. The novel gives us a psychological insight into the mind of an elderly woman suffering a religious crisis. ICS, partly due to his own complex and claustrophobic relationship with his mother, created some of the strongest female characters in modern literature; the old woman is an archetype in his writings, sometimes loving, sometimes ambiguous. The book posits, with absolute subtlety, the need for a compassionate, rather than a dogmatic, understanding of human needs: a message that is surely as important now as it ever was. (Kevin MacNeil)

The Coral Island
RM Ballantyne (1858)

Reading *The Coral Island* after a 40-year gap, I found I knew whole passages almost by heart. Had I read it that often? Ballantyne's stories, which began with his own adventures as an employee of the Hudson's Bay Company, successfully nourished generations of potential colonials, and the imperial message is plain. The depictions of the savages, who respond gratefully to Jack's civilising influence, hardened cannibals though they are, are highly suspect reading in the 21st century. The ultimate arrival of the missionary is not only perfunctory in terms of plot – clearly Ballantyne had had enough of his heroic trio at this point – but also ideologically disastrous. And yet the novel remains not only a gripping yarn, but is more ambiguous than I remembered.

Ballantyne was a master of plot. He borrowed unashamedly from Defoe and Wyss, but made their material his own. The discovery of the skeleton in the hut, the escape from the pirates by diving into the underwater cave and the shipwreck suspend disbelief, though details such as the penguins on this tropical island probably offend the more literal-minded.

At one point Peterkin, the junior member of the trio, addresses the cat: 'I love you because I've got to take care of you, and to look after you, and to think about you, and to see that you don't die.' Peterkin has real feelings about his castaway state, and a sense of irony which allows him, and the reader, to discern more than one meaning at

a time. The death of the cat, at the hands of the pirates, is the most upsetting moment in this novel full of human killings, because of Peterkin. By the end of the book he has grown up more than the two stuffed shirts ever will. (Margaret Elphinstone)

The Cutting Room
Louise Welsh (2002)

A host of successful new authors has sprung from Glasgow University's highly productive creative writing course over the last few years, with Louise Welsh at the front of the pack. *The Cutting Room* was Welsh's 2002 debut novel and it is a book that has quite rightly managed that tricky balance of garnering critical acclaim and achieving commercial success into the bargain. A literary crime novel, *The Cutting Room* has been an incredible success, winning umpteen prizes and awards, being translated into numerous languages, spawning a theatre production and with a big screen version (starring Robert Carlyle) currently in the making.

Much of the book's success is down to Welsh's incredible narrating character, Rilke. A cadaverous, gloomy, gay auctioneer, he drifts through the pages in acerbic, knowing fashion, a complex and instantly intriguing figure. Rilke discovers some disturbing old photographs while clearing out the house of a recently deceased old man, and as he tries to find out more about them he is sucked down into a murky world of pornographers, rent boys, drug dealers, transvestites and more, as events escalate dangerously out of control.

Welsh's handle on characterisation is brilliant, both with Rilke and the array of supporting deadbeats and no-hopers that populate the pages. But perhaps even more impressive is her depiction of Glasgow, as the city becomes a character in its own right; Gothic, dismal, decaying and frightening in equal measure. Using the crime novel format, Welsh does much more than tell a whodunnit story, employing the novel's backdrop to examine society's reaction to so-called sexual deviation, suggesting that what is and isn't acceptable is never a black and white issue, but rather a spectrum of shades of grey. A compelling and consuming read from start to finish, *The Cutting Room* is nothing short of an extraordinary debut. (Doug Johnstone)

A Day at the Office
Robert Alan Jamieson (1991)

'We should be free to wander,' says the unnamed narrator early on. And that's exactly what the author goes on to do. Pity

'Choose us. Choose life. Choose mortgage payments; choose washing machines; choose cars; choose sitting oan a couch watching mind-numbing and spirit-crushing game shows.'

Irvine Welsh's Trainspotting

While writing her second novel *The Little Friend*, Donna Tartt kept a photograph of her literary hero Robert Louis Stevenson on the wall by her desk.

the poor typesetter: each page of this book – a precursor to much modern experimental Scottish fiction – looks more like a work of art than a novel, with Jamieson jumping playfully in and out of italics, different fonts and size of lettering, punctuating the main text with succinct, sad mini-poems that are part interior monologue, part theory on life's big questions. Once you adjust your brain not to expect words in a straight line across the page, this style of delivery really helps an understanding of the text, almost as if each page has been opened up to reveal the layers of meaning contained within.

Though there is a plot of sorts, the story of Ray, Helen and Douglas (told upside-down, largely) isn't important. It hardly builds at all towards the end; instead, we get a subtle unravelling of each character. The tone is sympathetic to them all, slipping into their thoughts to explain often misguided actions, like when Ray is unsure whether to accept a flat being offered to him by a drug dealer, or when Helen walks out on her job.

There's nothing glamorous about Jamieson's portrayal of drug culture though, or what it's like to be poor, unemployed and frustrated. He is unflinching in his bleak descriptions of life on the dole, remaining interesting while simply describing picking up the giro and going straight to the bookies; proof you don't need sex or explosions to be intriguing. On the contrary, this kind of writing can be more rewarding, more truthful. And it is. *A Day at the Office* shows a healthy disrespect for the rules of language, but great economy with it. (Rodge Glass)

The Dear Green Place
Archie Hind (1966)

There are two kinds of books in this list: great fiction by people who happen to come from Scotland, and great fiction influenced by and composed with Scotland in mind. *The Dear Green Place* is perhaps the best example of the latter. From renditions of 'The Mist Covered Mountains' on the bagpipes, to the poetic refrain about the Glasgow coat-of-arms, to the unmistakable descriptions of its streets, rivers and buildings, the sense of place and time couldn't be stronger.

Set in the Southside of Glasgow of the 1960s, this is one of the few novels about writers and writing that actually contributes something fresh and different where most are simply self-indulgent. Mat Craig is from proud working-class stock, born into a large family who consider putting pen to paper as something shameful that should be

suppressed. The narrative swings between sections where Mat temporarily shelves his dreams to work with his brother in a slaughterhouse, and moments when he abandons employment in the name of literature: something he's not absolutely certain he believes in, or is any good at. Hind deals beautifully with questions of art over real life, juxtaposing the pull of creativity with Mat's inability to pay the bills, even succeeding in making the slitting, slashing and chopping of animals in the killing rooms seem romantic with his restrained tone.

The tragedy is not just in Mat's story, but also in that of the author. Hind too struggled with the ability and opportunity to write, and sadly never completed another book after this, his debut, was published in 1966. However, the contribution to Scottish life Mat struggles so hard for has been achieved by its creator in this impressive book which still stands as profound comment nearly 40 years on. And that's something to be proud of. (Rodge Glass)

A Disaffection
James Kelman (1989)

How Late it Was, How Late may have grabbed the headlines, *The Busconductor Hines* may have been more seminal, but it is *A Disaffection*, quietly, which is James Kelman's best book. Its 'hero' (a problematic term; it's James Kelman we're talking about) is Patrick Doyle, a single, bored English teacher. Each day he gently pines for a married colleague, clashes with his racist brother and fires frustrated polemic at his sixth-formers. Aware that he has succumbed to the rottenness of the system, disgusted by his employment as tool of the British state, he rebels in a most peculiar manner: by trying to fashion some old pipes into a musical instrument on which he can play the song of his sorrow. It is a symbol both of hope and the ridiculous.

Patrick stumbles through the novel's barren plains, searching for something, anything, that will help salve his pain, but makes no progress beyond endless cups of tea and stubbed out cigarettes. This book is a deep, slow, moving feast. Sceptics and supporters alike often reduce Kelman to his language, as if the ability to write in urban Scots is itself an achievement, but his real innovations lie elsewhere. Kelman captures the tremors and tempo of consciousness itself, immersing the reader in the yearning, futility and drained moments of hope in each hour of Patrick's world.

The characters in a Kelman novel are incarcerated not only in a socio-economic

1995 Royal Lyceum production,
photo Sean Hudson

The Gowk Storm

Nancy Brysson Morrison (1933)
Reviewer: Anne Donovan

The Gowk Storm is the story of three close-knit sisters, the daughters of a minister, living in a remote parish on the fringes of the Highlands. Narrated by Lisbet, the youngest sister, the novel is written mainly in English, but given a strong sense of place by the use of Scots words and some Scots dialogue. Lisbet describes the love affairs of her older sisters, Julia and Emmy, each of whom falls in love with a man deemed an unacceptable match by their patriarchal, rigid and prejudiced society.

The gowk storm of the title is 'a storm of several days at the end of April or beginning of May; an evil or abstract obstruction of short duration'. During the gowk storm, Julia's father discovers her with a lover, the dominie, sheltering in a hut. The community has recently become aware that he is Roman Catholic, and thus unsuitable. Their relationship echoes a gowk storm; he is forced to leave the parish while Julia marries the suitor preferred by her family. She is profoundly affected by the experience. A year later, another gowk storm is to have more tragic consequences for Emmy, who has violated the moral framework of society by falling in love with her friend's fiancé.

The Gowk Storm is one of the most atmospheric books I have ever read and the claustrophobia of the setting acts as a metaphor for the restrictions society places on these strong, intelligent and articulate young women. The symbolism of weather and the force of nature underpins the narrative. The weather is a character in itself, central to the main figures' lives; sometimes joyful, more often uncaring or malevolent, but always lovingly described and full of significance. What I love about the book is the detail; the way in which the author brings alive a character or place with economy and precision. The ferryman is 'a mere paring of a man', Christine Strathern's features are 'like a wax doll's which have melted ever so slightly at the fire'.

Lisbet, left at home when her sisters attend a party, studies the dregs of her milk: 'I looked at the milky castle peaks and milky brides at the bottom of the drained tumbler and at the skin, lined like a bat's wing, which clung to the side of the glass.' Haunting, lyrical, passionate and a real page-turner, *The Gowk Storm* is definitely one of my favourite Scottish novels.

Further reading: *Breakers* (1930) depicts three sisters trapped by convention and an oppressive existence in a Highland manse; *Mary Queen of Scots* (1960) beautifully imagines the life of the hapless monarch.

Anne Donovan
is the author of
Buddha Da and
Hieroglyphics.

Marlon Brando in *Apocalypse Now!*, adapted from Conrad, courtesy of BFI

Heart of Darkness
Joseph Conrad (1902)
Reviewer: Alexander McCall Smith

In the heyday of British Imperialism, *Blackwood's Magazine* in Edinburgh published a great number of stories of life and adventures in various colonial outposts. Much of this dated very quickly and is of only minor historical interest today. A novel serialised in the magazine in the late 19th century is a very striking exception. This was Joseph Conrad's *Heart of Darkness*, a work which is still the subject of lively debate today. Is it, as Chinua Achebe has suggested, a piece of Western condescension towards Africans? Or is it, as its supporters argue, a powerful indictment of Western imperialism?

I returned to this book last year after I had read *King Leopold's Ghost*, an extraordinary account by an American historian of the horrific exploitation of the Congo by the King of Belgium. Adam Hochschild, the author of this book, lays bare what amounted to a holocaust carried out by trading interests in the Congo, and produces hard facts and figures to make his point. Conrad's great novel, written with that marvellous, clear style, provides us with the feel of that time and place: the fear, the oppressive humidity, the bending river.

Reading it today, one feels that the book is entirely modern. There is none of the wordiness of so much late 19th century prose; just clear, uncluttered descriptions. And the sensibility, too, seems contemporary, almost that of an investigative journalist writing about what is happening in some tortured corner of Africa.

Heart of Darkness is a great novel for many different reasons. It is, first and foremost, an account of a great journey and a search for one man. As is true with any story of a quest – here for the legendary Mr Kurtz – the reader is anxious for the long-expected encounter. And then, when the person is found, we see only moral darkness and brutality. Behind all this is a lesson: we are surrounded by absurdity, madness and moral confusion. The social structures we create for ourselves may hold this at bay, but at times they do so only through hypocrisy and manipulation. If we comply with these structures, we may find ourselves serving cruel and rapacious goals; the Company's interest then; and what today: the interests of globalisation? *Heart of Darkness* is immensely unsettling, but perhaps we need to unsettle ourselves.

Further reading: *Nostromo* (1904) outlines the impact of foreign exploitation on a developing South American state; *The Secret Agent* (1907) is the 'simple tale' of Verloc, whose attempt to destroy an anarchist group goes disastrously awry.

Alexander McCall Smith *is the author of 55 books, including The No 1 Ladies Detective Agency, Portuguese Irregular Verbs, and The Sunday Philosophy Club. His new book, 44 Scotland Street, is published in March 2005, and his next book, Friends, Lovers, Chocolate, is published in September 2005.*

hell, but in their very existence. As such, Kelman becomes a novelist-philosopher in the tradition of Camus and Kafka, an experimentalist as redoubtable as Joyce or Beckett, and a writer who mines for the dignity in his characters even deeper than Steinbeck can. It is in *A Disaffection* that his vision is most complete: sad, human and vital. (Alan Bissett)

The Divided Self

See panel, page 16.

Docherty

William McIlvanney (1975)

Docherty is the most brilliant, forceful and yet measured example of William McIlvanney's desire to 'give working-class life the vote in the literature of heroism'. The struggles of the eponymous Docherty family in the early decades of the 20th century offer a microcosm of a broader working-class impulse towards emancipation and dignity. The central patriarch, Tam Docherty, embodies the west coast hardman tradition of Scottish writing; he's a miner whose own impulse to do the right thing often results in righteous and troubling violence.

Tam and his sons Conn, Michael and Angus all wrestle with inarticulacy, with a need to find an appropriate medium and language in which to express their experiences of hard industrial labour, grinding poverty, the horrors of war and the daily grind of working-class life. In a key scene, Conn is beaten in school for using Scots vernacular – supposedly the language of the gutter and an inappropriate medium for 'civilised' discourse in the classroom – a moment which neatly associates the imposition of Standard English with a kind of violence. Similarly, when Michael attempts to write to his family about the horrors he witnessed in World War I, he equates the lines on the page with the bars of a prison cage. As a whole, the novel crystallises a Scottish working-class circumspection that Standard English and standard literary forms are the adequate means of representing working-class experience.

Docherty stands as a piece of landmark fiction which appropriates the conventionally bourgeois form of the novel for highly radical purposes. Although Tam's life of trade unionism and struggle ends in tragedy, a clenched fist remains a potent symbol anticipating ongoing and future solidarity and change. However, the competitive individualism and self-serving disdain of Tam's son Angus also indicates

that this novel is not dewy-eyed sentimentalism but actually anticipates the fracture of working-class commonality which so colours Scottish writing from the 1980s to the present. (Aaron Kelly)

An Enquiry Concerning Human Understanding

David Hume (1748)

Only three years after the defeat of Bonnie Prince Charlie's troops at Culloden, a book was published that shattered the world of philosophy and paved the way for the Scottish Enlightenment. David Hume, then aged 37, recast the opening parts of his *Treatise of Human Nature* – which in his own words 'fell dead-born from the press' without reaching such distinction as even to excite a murmur among the zealots – as *An Enquiry Concerning Human Understanding*.

His aim was simple, if extensive. Hume set out to discover what ideas were, and how the mind used them. His conclusions unsettled centuries of presupposition. The details of his work on scepticism, causation and the non-existence of innate ideas are perhaps too technical to expand on here; however, his notorious section 'On Miracles' which he had excluded from the original *Treatise* amply shows the cast of his mind. He states that 'no testimony is sufficient to establish a miracle' unless 'its falsehood would be more miraculous than the fact'. The iconoclastic implications of this incontrovertible assertion become clear by the end of the essay: Christianity was at first attended by miracles, and it requires a similar miracle to believe in it now; 'mere reason is insufficient to convince us of its veracity: and whoever is moved by faith to assent to it, is conscious of a continued miracle in his own person, which subverts all the principles of his understanding.'

One cannot judge a philosopher like a multiple choice test, ticking or crossing his propositions. Hume's avowedly rational stance contains the seeds for Kant's critique of reason, and even Kierkegaard's existential theology. The *Enquiry*, with its knowing irony, brisk sanity and gloriously elegant prose, is more than the sum of its axioms. It is a testament to free-thinking, mental innovation and intellectual bravado. (Stuart Kelly)

Electric Brae

Andrew Greig (1992)

Throughout the 1990s, when the majority of the emerging Scottish novelists seemed fixated with gritty urban realism, a handful of authors were taking their inspiration

Oxford Philosophical Texts
The complete editions for students

David Hume

An Enquiry concerning Human Understanding

Edited by Tom L. Beauchamp

John Buchan's colourful non-literary life included a spell as Member of Parliament for Scottish Universities and he was appointed Governor-General of Canada in 1935.

from the dramatic landscape of the country's remoter climes. Notable among these was Andrew Greig, the Bannockburn-born poet, novelist and mountaineer, whose brilliant evocation of settings ranging from the Battle of Britain to colonial Penang across five novels has consistently matched his unnerving insight and compassion. Greig's debut novel *Electric Brae* is the most powerful evidence of the author's talent for conveying the intricacies of human relationships against a vividly realised physical and political backdrop. The author himself described the book as 'a modern romance without heather or hardmen'.

Greig's protagonist is Jimmy Renilson, an engineer aboard a North Sea oil rig, who divides his time between an affair with temperamental artist Kim Russell and rock climbing (the latter, a passion he shares with the book's author). Greig's extraordinarily dense and fast-paced narrative moves between Jimmy's stormy relationship with Kim and the predicaments among their wider circle of friends such as Jimmy's climbing friend Graeme and his bisexual partner Lesley. Despite somewhat bleak subject matter, Greig's no-holds-barred depiction of the near impossibility of intimacy between men and women is balanced by the sensitivity he extends to his characters.

The action expands to take in the effects of Thatcher's compassionless conservatism on the Scottish nation, also strongly evoked, while the mountaineering sequences are elegantly, energetically conveyed. *Electric Brae* features the density, scope and page-turning intensity of a true modern epic and there are surely few contemporary novelists who can explore the big themes of love, death and loss in language that is so spare and beautiful. (Allan Radcliffe)

The Expedition of Humphry Clinker
Tobias Smollett (1771)
Tobias Smollett's last and best novel is misleadingly named. Clinker – a comically over-enthusiastic Scottish manservant – does not appear until a third of the way through the book, and is often conspicuous by his absence. Instead, the central figure is Matt Bramble, a grumpy member of the Welsh landed gentry, who takes his family and assorted hangers-on on a trip around Britain. The journey is supposedly for the good of his health, but much of what he sees – patrons of Bath's spas bathing in each other's waters, Londoners mixing in a

relentless mess and Edinburgh's common stairwells dripping with effluent – puts him in a foul temper.

Born near Dumbarton in 1721, much of Smollett's writing (he was a journalist and a surgeon as well as a novelist) was characterised by this scurrilous negativity and obsession with disease. Alongside high points such as the bestselling picaresque *The Adventures of Roderick Random* and *A Complete History of England*, Smollett was imprisoned for three months for libel. His health, never strong, encouraged him to move to Italy, where he wrote *Clinker*, dying months after its publication. The work shows a certain mellowing in the irascible author. Bramble's is the dominant voice, but Smollett's use of the epistolary form allowed him to introduce the views of varying associates: his cocky nephew Jery, naive niece Liddy and barely literate maid Win. These accounts contradict and qualify each other in a sparky narrative mesh. The result is that, for all its wicked satire and gruesome comedy, *Humphry Clinker* is a warm and engaging novel.

Its grotesque, caricatured social climbers illustrate Smollett's conservatism, while its praise of Scotland as an example to the rest of Britain echoes his unionism. But this ideology is never overpowering. Today, among a host of 18th century classics that seem ponderous in the extreme, its pungent descriptions, clever dramatic irony and broad humour are well worth relishing. (James Smart)

Flemington
Violet Jacob (1911)
Flemington is a finely wrought historical adventure written by a poet. It belongs to a Scottish tradition reaching from Scott through Stevenson and Buchan, who described *Flemington* as 'the best Scots romantic novel since *The Master of Ballantrae*'. This book is distinctive by being rooted in Angus and its location makes it an important regional novel; Montrose was strongly Jacobite and the House of Balnillo in the book is based on the House of Dun which belonged to Violet Jacob's family. An intimate sense of landscape based on knowledge of place, character and speech pervades the novel.

Jacob combines poetic sensibility with clear structure, action and pace. This makes *Flemington* an accomplished demonstration of appropriate form, animated by prose of a high quality: 'He was almost in darkness, for the port looked northward, and the pale light barely glimmered through it, but he could just see a spurt of white leap into the

Courtesy of Getty Images

Hotel World
Ali Smith (2001)
Reviewer: Zoë Strachan

'Wooooooooohooooooo what a fall what a soar what a plummet what a dash into dark into light . . .' So opens *Hotel World*, as Sara Wilby's ghost remembers her body plunging to its death down a lift shaft in a branch of the Global Hotel chain. Right away we know we're in for a rollercoaster narrative. 'I want to make a book so strong you can hit it with a hammer and it doesn't fall apart,' Ali Smith said once in an interview. I haven't tested it with the tool kit, but *Hotel World* may just be that book.

Its grand themes and grimy details grow with re-reading. Characters skip between the six sections as Smith switches voices with awesome ease. Nothing is introduced then ignored; no images are left to fester, forgotten. Falling, for example: homeless Else letting fall vowels ('Spr sm chng?'); Lise the receptionist falling mysteriously ill; the Penny dropping for a jaded journo as she remembers her parachute jump; grief-stricken Clare imagining her sister diving from the highest board at the swimming pool; the assistant in a watch repair shop falling in love with a customer. Readers fall, too; for Smith's characters and their world, haunted by their presence long after the covers have closed on their stories.

Smith grew up in Scotland, and I like to think her work is rooted in our great tradition of the fantastic. She utterly disregards boring notions of reality. Ghosts? Metaphysical poet-quoting homeless people? Why the

hell not? As Smith gently reminds us – 'Here's the story' – it *is* a story. Unlike many writers, she doesn't consider literary theory in the way M Night Shyamalan's villagers viewed the Shed That Must Not Be Entered. She's happy to open the door and have a rummage around, as if it's the Left Behind Room of the Global Hotel, and her experiments with language and structure never sacrifice readability. Every page, every line, every word is packed with substance, but substance always matches style.

The adjectives which Penny uses to describe the global could be applied afresh to the novel. Superior! Transcendent! *Hotel World* makes you want to seize with both hands its suggestion to 'remember you must live'. If the world's a hotel, make the most of it before you check out. Wooooohoooooooo!

Further reading: Smith's greatest strength is in her richly imaginative short stories, so try *Other Stories and Other Stories* (1999) and *The Whole Story and Other Stories* (2003).

Zoë Strachan
*is the author of
Negative Space and
Spin Cycle.*

Basil Rathbone in the 1939 film adaptation

The Hound of the Baskervilles
Arthur Conan Doyle (1902)
Reviewer: Margaret Elphinstone

'Mr Holmes, they were the footprints of a gigantic hound!'

I have read my copy of *The Hound of the Baskervilles* so many times that the pages have gone soft with much turning, but Dr Mortimer's words to Holmes never fail to thrill me. This is where Arthur Conan Doyle achieves the perfect balance between rational deduction and the terrors of the Gothic subtext. No amount of empirical reasoning can make Baskerville Hall a homely spot (even though Sir Henry starts stripping the creeping ivy off the mullioned windows), or tame the wild corners of Dartmoor, let alone penetrate to the terrifying heart of the Grimpen Mire. Even though we start with one of those enviable breakfasts in 221B Baker Street, and end up comfortably by the fire on a November evening, the ghosts encountered in the West Country are not entirely banished. The London fog still lurks outside the window, and Sir Henry's health is broken by his encounter with uncanny forces.

Holmes himself is an equivocal figure, as he hides out on the moor alongside a maniacal convict and a luminous hound. Like the hound, he prefers to act by moonlight. Like the convict, he uses a Neolithic stone hut as his secret lair: the suggestion of a remote and savage ancestry is applied not only to those who belong on the moor, but to the sophisticated Londoners who have come to solve this rural mystery. It is the inimical fog, not the human villain, which nearly defeats Holmes.

Paradoxically, this is a great detective story because it defies its own genre. On the first page, Holmes observes Watson's actions reflected in the coffee pot on the breakfast table; deduction, he remarks, is always prosaic when the logic is made explicit. Detective stories tend to reassure the reader that reason can and will overcome evil, but *The Hound* does nothing of the sort. Watson sets out to 'make the reader share those dark fears and vague surmises which clouded our lives so long, and ended in so tragic a manner'. The arrest of Stapleton is nicely contrived, but it doesn't do much to allay the dark fears. Holmes thinks best in a 'room filled with smoke' from 'the acrid fumes of strong, coarse tobacco'. The detective, in fact, is as equivocal a figure as the hound; by occupation, indeed, he is one himself. This is the perfect detective story because nothing is quite as simple as the light of reason makes it seem.

Further reading: *A Study in Scarlet* (1887), the first Holmes mystery, opens with a bloody murder in Brixton; *The Lost World* (1913) introduces Professor George Edward Challenger.

Margaret Elphinstone *is the author of eight books, including* Voyageurs, Hy Brasil, *and* The Sea Road. *Her new book,* Gato, *is published in March 2005, and her next book,* Light, *is published in 2006.*

air midway across the channel, where a second shot had struck the water. As he rushed on deck a puff of smoke was dispersing above Dial Hill. Then another cloud rolled from the bushes on the nearest point of Inchbrayock Island, and he felt the Venture shiver and move in her moorings.'

Thematically, *Flemington* reworks the classic conflict of Whig versus Jacobite in religious, political and psychological terms. Humanity is obscured by warring factions, but not lost because Jacob grounds these divisions in rounded and convincing character studies. Flemington himself is a divided yet humane protagonist, moving amidst a subtly portrayed rogues' gallery that includes Skirling Wattie, a dogged local survivor, the formidable plotter Christine Flemington, and the evasive, self-interested landowner David Balnillo. *Flemington* is a brightly faceted jewel in the literary crown, richly coloured, resonant with poetic depths, and intensely readable. (Donald Smith)

For the Love of Willie
Agnes Owens (1998)
It is often remarked that Scottish scribes have a particular proclivity for mining the dark and devilish in their fiction. Agnes Owens' *For the Love of Willie* displays all the pitch-black humour and acute observation that have characterised her work since her debut *Gentlemen of the West*.

For the Love of Willie starts out in a mental institution where patient Peggy is attempting to enlist the proofreading skills of fellow resident 'the Duchess'. Initially reluctant, she is soon drawn into the tale of Peggy's early life in a small west of Scotland town. At the heart of the story is Peggy's brief and unexpected affair with her employer, Willie, with whom she falls madly in love. Initially imagining that her lover is going to leave his wife for her, Peggy is soon abandoned, pregnant, shamed and forced to fall back on her mother to make decisions about her future.

Owens has a reputation as one of Scotland's least assuming literary figures who consistently applies her eye for the quietly bizarre and ear for the bad and bitchy to the everyday and familiar. *Gentlemen of the West*, for instance, evolved from the colourful tales of the building trade she picked up from her husband and son. *For the Love of Willie* is her most accomplished work because it combines such energetic observation with an exploration of some of the most painful and difficult questions regarding love,

female sexuality and repression. Not bad for a mother of seven from Balloch who joined a creative writing group because it meant 'a night away from the kids'. (Allan Radcliffe)

From Russia With Love
Ian Fleming (1957)
'My name is Bond, James Bond.' There are few characters of the 20th century that can boast the kind of global renown of Ian Fleming's British secret agent. Widely regarded as the best of Fleming's novels (JFK rated it among his top ten favourite books) *From Russia With Love* centres on a plot by SMERSH (the Russian organisation dedicated to wiping out foreign spies) to murder 007 in as ignominious circumstances as possible to ensure maximum embarrassment for the British Secret Service. Under the watchful eyes of Colonel Rosa Klebb, a trap is laid in Istanbul with a code machine and the delectable Tatiana Romanova as bait and the sociopathic Red Grant as the assassin in waiting.

What is striking about Fleming's work is its economy; in all his novels there is a strict linear pattern, no extraneous characters and a merciful lack of unnecessary subplots to pad out the proceedings. Like chess pieces, the characters are carefully placed on the board before they are moved toward their inevitable conclusions. Fleming has a wonderful way with characterisation, with each individual an integral part of the plot and given a comprehensive expression of emotions and mannerisms. The level of detail that is dedicated to each one lifts *From Russia With Love* to such a degree that there is a sense of humanity even in Klebb and Grant, two of the more grotesque Bond villains.

For those whose only experience of Bond is through the silver screen, you are in for an altogether different experience. Written in 1957, this is a lean, atmospheric Cold War thriller. Starting in Moscow and culminating in a taut four-day journey from Istanbul to Paris on the Orient Express, it is spectacular entertainment that is only heightened by Hollywood's bastardisation of Fleming's work. (Gordon Eldrett)

The Game of Kings
Dorothy Dunnett (1962)
Dorothy Dunnett started writing books having complained to her husband that she had run out of things to read. Her debut, *The Game of Kings*, appeared at the end of 18 months fuelled by the extensive research

'So it was she knew she liked him, loved him as they said in the soppy English books, you were shamed and a fool to say that in Scotland.'
Lewis Grassic Gibbon's Sunset Song

that would characterise all of her historical novels. Set in Scotland at the height of the Renaissance – in the aftermath of the disastrous loss to the English at the Battle of Pinkie – the novel follows Francis Crawford, Master of Lymond, who has been judged a traitor and disowned by his family and friends. He sneaks back into Scotland to assume leadership of his notorious band of mercenaries and pursue his own agenda across the taut political chessboard of the Scottish Borders.

The adventures of this brilliant, elegant and deeply flawed hero make for compulsive reading, as he plays a devastating game within the complex, confusing, tense and corrupt world of 16th century Scotland. The society which Lymond scandalises is peopled with a broad diversity of completely real characters, each with their own agendas, prejudices and beliefs, and all fighting to hold onto what they love most dearly, be it home, wealth, power, nation or family.

It has been said, numerous times, that this book changed the course of historical fiction. Effortlessly accurate and real, anchored in actual events, Dunnett's work brings the time to life with a vivacity and wit unsurpassed in the genre. It challenges the reader to keep up; with the speed and complexity of the plot, with the brilliance of language and the wordplay, with the richness of the setting and the riotousness of its characters. But most of all *The Game of Kings* makes 16th century Scotland and its people real, tangible and thoroughly absorbing. (Philippa Cochrane)

Garnethill
Denise Mina (1998)
There was a time when the Glasgow-set detective story meant little more than the adventures of one craggy-faced chief inspector, handy with his fists, the originator of that oft-recited catchphrase: 'There's been a murrrder . . . ' From the late 90s, however, when a clutch of Scottish crime writers began garnering attention for innovations within the genre, Denise Mina achieved instant success for her striking depiction of the city's dark criminal underbelly, *Garnethill*.

On one level, the novel certainly adheres to generic conventions, with an urgent investigation into a grisly death at its heart. Mina's reluctant detective is Maureen O'Donnell, graduate with distinction from the school of hard knocks who, having survived an abusive childhood, a spell in psychiatric care and the unwelcome interventions of her

dysfunctional family, lives in splendid isolation, surveying the dear green place from atop a tenement in Garnethill. Her brief peace is unceremoniously shattered when her lover, a psychiatrist with secrets of his own, is murdered in her flat, while Maureen lies passed out drunk in the bedroom. Harassed by the police, Maureen sets out to find her own answers, the investigation bringing her into contact with a memorable collection of invidious lowlifes.

Inevitably, a brief synopsis cannot do justice to Mina's novel. As well as being a compelling tale, the book is remarkable for its vivid, imaginative evocation of the cityscape as viewed from Maureen's self-imposed exile at one of the city's highest points. Also striking is the blackly funny tone, and the warmth Mina extends to her characters. Drunks, drug-dealers and petty criminals are revealed to have complex motivations, while Maureen herself is a marvellous creation, compassionate and vulnerable as well as bold and tenacious. (Allan Radcliffe)

The Golden Bough
James Frazer (1890)
Though largely debunked as anthropology, the legacy of James Frazer's *The Golden Bough* remains incalculable. Tracing humanity's belief in magic through religion to scientific rationality, across a staggering array of ancient and developing cultures, this fiercely ambitious, heavyweight tome had a seismic impact on Western thought when first published. Never mind that the Cambridge don never witnessed any of the tribal rituals he wrote so eloquently about, cobbling his theories – principally those of primitive worship and periodic sacrifice of a sacred king – together from second-hand traveller and missionary accounts.

And no matter that after expanding his book to a massive 12 volumes, the subsequent abridged version excised his controversial implication of Jesus' fictitiousness. This was literary dynamite, profoundly influencing many of the great modernist writers, including Yeats, Joyce, Lawrence, Pound and Plath. Freud and Jung argued at length about it. TS Eliot cited it as a major inspiration for *The Wasteland*, though Frazer himself couldn't see it. And the impression it made on George Lucas' mythological mentor Joseph Campbell was such that the book arguably laid the groundwork for *Star Wars*.

Born in Glasgow in 1854, at age 15 Frazer enrolled at the university to study classical literature. After graduating, he

The House with the Green Shutters

George Douglas Brown (1901)
Reviewer: Laura Marney

Oh God, what was I thinking? Why did I sign up to review a book that has a boring title, is more than 100 years old, was a one-hit wonder, and is beloved of crusty old academics who boff on about its model of classical Greek tragedy? It's got to be mince, yeah? Until George Douglas Brown's book, Scotland's rural communities had been represented in a style known as kailyard (or cabbage patch). These were cutesy heather and haggis havens of holistic wholesomeness. Then along came *The House with the Green Shutters* (the *Trainspotting* of its day), giving the kailyard a well-deserved kick in the chuckies.

This was an angry young man's response to the misrepresentation of contemporary Scottish life and the industrial and spiritual changes taking place. GDB skilfully lulls the reader by beginning with the traditional kailyard format and then subverts it with vicious humour into a deliciously ruthless portrayal of small-town petty jealousies. It's semi-autobiographical, probably based on Ochiltree in Ayrshire, where Brown grew up. He was illegitimate and rejected by his father and this perhaps explains the demonic father figure. The main protagonist, John Gourlay, the town's feared and fearless merchant, emasculates the townsmen making them merely 'bodies': gossipy old women. He despises his own spineless son and when he is unable to adapt to the arrival of the railway his hubris becomes the family's downfall.

The right book at absolutely the right time, it was a bestseller. Not every bestseller is a classic but every classic is a bestseller and this scores on both points. It's up there with Balzac, Flaubert and others who created the best of European literature. George Douglas Brown himself called it a 'brutal and bloody work', but although by the end there is a body count to rival Tarantino, it's a fun book. There is a sly, dark humour in every aspect of the characterisation, the dialogue and analysis. Its insight into human nature and the tragedy of wasted potential is what makes it timeless.

So impressed were the press at the time they could hardly believe it was only his second novel. OK, it was a long time ago and the reviews are a bit dusty now but a good book remains a good book and through time can achieve, as *The House with the Green Shutters* has quietly done, the status of a great read.

Further reading: *Love and a Sword* (1899) is his only other completed novel, an adventure story for boys originally published under the pseudonym Kennedy King.

Laura Marney *is the author of No Wonder I Take a Drink. Her new book, Nobody Loves a Ginger Baby, is published in June 2005.*

King James Bible: Authorised Version
Various (1611)
Reviewer: Richard Holloway

Christ of St John of the Cross
by Salvador Dali, courtesy of
Glasgow Museum of Religion

It was the only memorable and enduring thing that came out of the Hampton Court Conference of 1604, which was called to consider the demands of the Puritans for the reform of the Church of England. King James I or VI, depending on which side of the Border you're on, presided. The Puritans wanted the English bishops brought to heel: James was having none of it. Having gratefully escaped from the religious strife of Scotland, he didn't want a re-run in England: 'Nae bishop, nae king', was his curt dismissal of that move. It was different when one of the Puritans present at the conference, John Rainolds, president of Corpus Christi College Cambridge, suggested that there should be a new translation of the Bible. James ordered that the work should start immediately. He established a group of 50 translators who sat in six groups, two at Oxford, two at Cambridge, and two at Westminster. The work started in 1607 and took two years and nine months to complete. Each man got 30 shillings a week for undertaking the noble work.

Strictly speaking it is not a new translation. The preface of the translators states that it's a revision that tries to steer a course between earlier Puritan and Roman Catholic versions. It is also incorrect to call it the 'Authorised Version', for authorised it never was. Rather it was 'appointed to be read in churches', as the title page still states. All that aside, it remains one of the enduring triumphs of the English language, up there with the great tragedies of Shakespeare, which were written at exactly the same time. We are used to identifying and celebrating the genius of an individual like Shakespeare: how can we account for the genius of a committee of 50, albeit one that contained a number of supremely gifted men?

Adam Nicolson, in his book on the subject, claims that Shakespeare's great tragedies and the *King James Bible* are each other's mirror-twin, with both emerging from the ambitions and terrors of the Jacobean world. However we explain the achievement, the *King James Bible* is one of the glories of the world, unique because its beauty and power appeal to believer and unbeliever alike. In the words of the Epistle to the Hebrews: 'It is quick and powerful and sharper than any two-edged sword, piercing even to the dividing asunder of soul and spirit, and of the joints and marrow, and is a discerner of the thoughts and intents of the heart.'

Further reading: James VI & I is also the author of *Daemonologie* (1597); *The True Lawe of Free Monarchies* (1598); and *Basilicon Doron* (1599).

Richard Holloway *is the author of 25 books including Doubts and Loves, Godless Morality, and Looking in the Distance.*

won a scholarship to Trinity College, Cambridge, where he lived almost uninterrupted till his death. His masterpiece, *The Golden Bough*, has been in and out of critical fashion but always in print, seminal to the growth of anthropology as a science and the social study of myth. Taking a mere 17-word, classical Greek story of successive warrior-priests slain by a divine branch at the woodland lake of Nemi in Italy, Frazer concocted a monumental prose-poem and entire history of human belief. His imaginative matrix of cultural connectivity rather than any great investigative rigour has ensured his posterity. (Jay Richardson)

The Gowk Storm

See panel, page 19.

Grace Notes

Bernard MacLaverty (1997)

Writing outside the gender barrier is a tough business. There's always the risk that the relationship between author and subject strays too close to that of puppeteer and marionette. To attempt this creative leap demonstrates a writer's confidence in his craft. To land it takes great skill; a jeweller's eye for gesture and an ear fine-tuned to variations in voice. In *Grace Notes*, Bernard MacLaverty made that leap and landed to the applause of critics and readers which resonated to his shortlisting for the Booker Prize.

MacLaverty's work is always challenging, from the disturbing story of a man's attempt to save a boy in *Lamb*, through the troubled tale of love across the barricades that is *Cal*, to the bittersweet laughter in a journey through friendship and final exams in *The Anatomy Lesson*. In *Grace Notes*, MacLaverty introduces Catherine McKenna, a complex woman, composer and single mother whose estrangement from her family augments her deepening depression. She has returned to Belfast to bury her father and face her mother. Catherine brings back secrets, which MacLaverty uses with deft precision to draw the reader through the novel, gently tugging skeletons out of the closet, one bony knuckle at a time, giving us the grace behind disgrace.

Catherine and MacLaverty have much in common. Born in Belfast before settling in Scotland, and a profession in teaching given up in pursuit of their arts are shared between writer and character. Still, this does not account for the most gripping moments when Catherine is giving birth or experiencing emotions she believes no mother should be made to endure. The brilliance of *Grace Notes* cannot be attributed to a single element, but lies in subtleties of shade and tone found throughout. Music is paramount. It pulses in a rhythm through each line. Elegant. Beautifully phrased. Pitch perfect. (Will Napier)

Greenvoe

George Mackay Brown (1972)

Transposing the Orcadian rhythms of his critically-acclaimed poetry to a prose work which focuses on the dissipation of an island community proved a masterstroke for George Mackay Brown. In the absence of any real plot, we find ourselves embroiled in the lives of the inhabitants of Greenvoe, a village on the fictional island of Hellya, constructing the greater truths of their lives from the minutiae of petty conflict and amity in their relationships. This is all threatened with the arrival of Black Star, a secret military project which causes a boom economy in the village before the inevitable bust, and a descent into ochlocracy.

The majority of the action takes place over a single week, watching the fortunes of an ensemble cast that would make Robert Altman blush ebb and flow with the island tides. Transcending the parochial setting to reveal a parable about the impact of ultra-modern technology on a primitive society, Brown warily circles the rural sentimentality of the kailyard school but is never content with its cloying simplicity. And although undoubtedly a better poet than he was a novelist, in his works of elegiac social realism the islands of Orkney themselves are transformed into a mythological landscape worthy of the Norse sagas which influenced his work.

His poetry and prose, the latter of which perhaps never reached the heights of *Greenvoe* again, drew a bridge between Orkney – Norwegian territory until 1470 – and the Scottish mainland, uniting two traditions in lyrical paeans to the beauty and cruelty of island life. For a hint as to how much Brown's debut novel has been assimilated into the fabric of Orcadia, Northlink Ferries named one of the bars on their vessel Hamnavoe after it, a gesture the hard-drinking Bard of Orkney would surely have tipped a glass to. (Dave Martin)

The Guns of Navarone

Alistair MacLean (1957)

It will doubtless surprise many to find this most pulp of World War II action-adventures included in a compendium of Scotland's most accomplished fiction. But

Catherine Carswell studied at both the Conservatory of Music in Frankfurt and at Glasgow University but, because women were not formally admitted to the University at the time, was never awarded a degree.

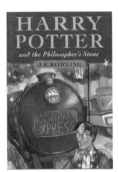

cast out Gregory Peck and J Lee Thompson's plodding, waterlogged film adaptation from your tainted minds and savour instead Alistair MacLean's utterly compelling source novel. Typically, MacLean doesn't waste time scene-setting before plunging his readers into the thick of the action. In essence, the plot concerns a suicide mission to sabotage two notorious German gun posts on an impregnable cliff in occupied Greece. Rather like animated super-family *The Incredibles*, each of MacLean's five-strong team has some individual skill to contribute to the mission, from Captain Keith Mallory's boast to be the world's greatest rock climber to the sailing expert and alpine wanderer Andy Stevens.

Naturally, their assignment is punctuated with regular obstacles, most memorably the moment when our heroes seem on the verge of discovery, only to blow up an enemy boat with two conveniently at hand boxes of explosives. Yes, MacLean's characters are thinly sketched, the dialogue stilted and the occasional moralistic proselytising difficult to square with such evident glee at the violent, action set-pieces. Yet, the exhilarating narrative drive is in keeping with MacLean's self-effacing assertion: 'I'm a storyteller. There's no art in what I do, no mystique.'

One of the world's most commercially successful authors, MacLean was in fact as Scottish as black bun and *The Broons*. Born in Glasgow, the son of a Presbyterian minister, he spent his early childhood in the Highlands, near Inverness, speaking Gaelic at home. Intriguingly therefore, MacLean is one of the tiny band of authors on this list for whom English was a second language. (Allan Radcliffe)

Harry Potter and the Philosopher's Stone
JK Rowling (1997)

Before the Empire – the midnight queues round the block, the merchandise, the films and 800-page sequels – there was *The Philosopher's Stone*. It's easy to forget just what a phenomenon it is, and why. The story begins with Hagrid taking an 11-year-old Harry away to Hogwarts, the school of magic where he'll learn how special he is, all about his parents, and meet friends Ron and Hermione, with whom he will have all his adventures. On the way to the story's dramatic conclusion in the last chamber, we learn about Quidditch, Gryffindor, Voldemort and, finally, the frightening Man With Two Faces; but though it races along excitingly and is written well, it's hard to

judge the story alone any more, independent of all that has now become Potterworld.

When this book was first published, it was not with the kind of fanfare that those arriving in its wake have come to expect; it wasn't even expected to sell 10,000 copies, far less the millions it now has. And it's worth remembering that the publishers were completely unprepared for what happened. *The Philosopher's Stone* was a rare word-of-mouth success; a true literary phenomenon. Nobody could have predicted it. It sold what it sold and became what it became because children read it, loved it and were inspired to pass it to their friends, their parents (until recently, a rare thing) and to go on to read other, less accessible books.

It was powerful enough to change the way we think about children's fiction, and to turn a whole generation back on to the power of imagination, of magic, the joy of reading. For that alone we should be thankful. Whether this book sits as comfortably in this list in another hundred years remains to be seen, but right now it certainly deserves its place. (Rodge Glass)

Heart of Darkness
See panel, page 20.

The Highland Clearances
John Prebble (1969)

Although born in Middlesex, John Prebble grew up in Sutherland, a town in the Canadian province of Saskatchewan. It was amongst the descendants of Scottish emigrants – offspring of the crofters who had been forced to leave the Highlands by landlords intent on using land for sheep farming – that he first drank in Scotland's history. In his autobiography he describes his primary school teacher Miss Campbell: 'Although [she] had never been to Scotland, she spoke of it with an intense pride . . . telling us about that far land of mist and mountain [which] was in so great a contrast to the familiar world about us, the wide and treeless prairie.'

Through his RAF service during World War II and a subsequent spell as a journalist, he went where Miss Campbell had not. His relationship with Scotland grew through a sense of injustice at a mythical world lost. For although *The Highland Clearances* is packed with superb characterisation and finely wrought dramatic moments (Prebble wrote the screenplay for *Zulu* around the same time), his indignation overtakes his dedication to the truth. 'He was coal and

Courtesy of Canongate Books

Lanark
Alasdair Gray (1981)
Reviewer: Ron Butlin

Alasdair Gray's *Lanark* is one of the finest novels written in English. Its unique blend of realism and wild surrealism was greeted with great acclaim when it was first published, especially abroad. In France, for example, it sold out within four weeks and had to be immediately reprinted. In the US, it was originally marketed as sci-fi and flopped: *Lanark* is no more sci-fi than is the work of Dante or Blake. American publishers rebranded it for their second edition, and it is now recognised there as a major 20th century classic. In Scotland, it towers over all other contemporary fiction.

Arranged in four books, the novel opens with Book Three, set in the ever-darkening Unthank, a city not so far removed, spiritually speaking, from Glasgow. Here, in a wonderfully evoked present-day hell, Lanark emerges – a man without a past, it seems – to begin his search for love in a loveless place. Time and again he tries to remember the concept 'hope'; even the memory of 'dawn' takes on a near-heartbreaking poignancy. The message is clear: the more Lanark refuses to be crushed, the greater will be his suffering.

Books One and Two are realistic, set in post-war Glasgow. In straightforward flashback they relate the very Scottish upbringing of young Duncan Thaw and his subsequent struggles as a would-be artist. Struggles that end in tragedy. Gradually we learn that Duncan Thaw and Lanark are two stages of the same person, a kind of death and resurrection. Then, with an almost miraculous

inevitability, the novel begins to fit together. The whole works magnificently, carrying us from the personal to the universal, culminating in a searing satire that is surely one of the finest political allegories ever penned.

Thanks to the power of Gray's vision, image becomes narrative, allowing him to tell a greater truth than mere events. The dragonhide, the mouths, the flesh-eating are perfect metaphors for what it is to be human; Unthank *is* sunless Glasgow, and the psychological and spiritual darkness is real and physical. *Lanark* is a masterpiece and, though very serious, it is also very, very funny. At one point the author himself appears and is asked to explain himself. Most of all, it is a testament to the human spirit. Alasdair Gray shows us the moral courage that is our only hope in this increasingly despairing world.

Further reading: *1982, Janine* (1984) is one night in the life and lonely sexual fantasies of Jock McLeish; *Poor Things* (1993) is a feminist reworking of the Frankenstein myth.

Ron Butlin *is the author of nine books including The Sound of My Voice, Night Visits, and Vivaldi and the Number 3. His new books, No More Angels and Without a Backward Glance, are published in 2005.*

James Boswell by George Willison,
The Scottish National Portrait Gallery

The Life of Samuel Johnson
James Boswell (1791)
Reviewer: Bella Bathurst

It may seem a strange thing to rate an author who begins his masterpiece with a famous demurral of his own country ('I do indeed come from Scotland, but I cannot help it') as one of Scotland's greatest writers. But still, there it is; James Boswell's *The Life of Samuel Johnson* is one of the great classics of literature, and deservedly so.

For a long time, received wisdom considered it a work of genius written by an idiot. As Walter Scott put it, the book, 'though one of the most entertaining in the world, is not just what one would wish a near relation to have written'. Why? Well, mainly because it was honest. In detailing Johnson's silly walks and old deformities, Boswell destroyed the notion of biographical subjects as distant heroic paragons. By recording his drunken outbursts and his melancholia, Boswell offered an image of his subject which was just too vivid, too tactile, too real for many readers. And by proving that Johnson had valued Boswell both as a friend and future biographer, Boswell provided proof for his critics that even Johnson was capable of making misjudgements. The only evidence he was unable to provide was the most obvious of all: the book explained why Boswell needed Johnson, but not why Johnson needed Boswell.

With time, however, the book's flaws have become its strengths. Reading it now, 214 years after it was first published, it is still possible to be delighted and outraged by Boswell's methodology. He could be thorough, knowing, scandalous, empathic, generous, funny,

meticulous, absurd, indiscreet, hagiographic, frank and touching. He could also be a fabulous writer. *The Life of Samuel Johnson* earns its place not only because it is the definitive work on its subject, or because it is the first and greatest of modern biographies, or because it forever gives the lie to the literary dogma that fiction is somehow superior to non-fiction, but because everyone knows a Johnson, and everyone knows a Boswell.

Everyone has, at some stage in their lives, encountered just that same conjunction of personalities; the guru and the disciple, the boss and the deputy, the artist and the hanger-on, the been-there and the wannabe. And because, flitting almost unnoticed through its pages is something both quieter and stronger; the story of a friendship, a mutual dependency, and the bond between two flawed and brilliant men.

Further reading: *An Account of Corsica* (1768) includes a celebrated meeting with leader General Paoli; *Journal of a Tour to the Hebrides* (1784) revisits Boswell and Johnson's 1770s Highlands tour.

Bella Bathurst *is the author of* The Lighthouse Stevensons *and* Special. *Her new book,* The Wreckers: A Story of Killing Seas, False Lights and Plundered Shipwrecks, *is published in April 2005.*

wool joined by a stately hyphen and ennobled by five coronets,' writes Prebble of George Granville Leveson-Gower, First Duke of Sutherland, before casting him as a villain.

That Sutherland paid people to clear his lands is true, but as later historians such as Eric Richards have shown, Sutherland's wife, a native Scot, was the prime mover in the area's 'improvement'. Writing in his autobiography, published in 1993, Prebble excuses himself and explains why his book has an enduring appeal. 'I wish I had been able to read [Richard's history] 30 years ago when I was writing my own and when to my knowledge, no academic was taking an interest in the Clearances, systematic or cinematic.' (Tim Abrahams)

Hotel World
See panel, page 23.

The Hound of the Baskervilles
See panel, page 24.

The House with the Green Shutters
See panel, page 27.

Imagined Corners
Willa Muir (1931)
Willa Muir may be one of the lesser known names on this list, but that's due more to her date of birth (and perhaps her husband's name) than her undoubted talent. One of Scotland's foremost feminists, a brilliant, experimental psychology student and founder member of the Women's Students Suffrage Society long before such a thing was acceptable, Muir spent her life fighting for women's causes. Yet she was curiously conservative when it came to speaking out in favour of her own writing, which was largely ignored at the time of release.

Perhaps inevitable comparisons with her husband, the great Scottish poet Edwin Muir, led her to question the quality of her own literary contribution. Or perhaps, despite her progressive views, she felt obliged to play the part of loyal poet's wife and translator of others' work above that of independent voice: she only wrote two novels and a handful of academic pieces. But *Imagined Corners* alone represents a major contribution to Scottish literature, and we should be grateful for its existence. It is the most successful drawing together of all the issues Muir spent her life fighting for.

Set in the village of Calderwick (as is all her fiction) – an inward-looking,

prejudiced, chauvinist village somewhere in Scotland – every line shows Muir's frustration with her nation, but also a total preoccupation with it. In her calm, subtle, eloquent style, through two typically quiet but tough female characters, she tells us the story of Elise Mutze and Elisabeth Shand. Elise is free of the expectations of male-dominated society while Elisabeth realises herself only after becoming free of Hector, a man she thought she loved but was merely expected to. 'In loving Hector,' Muir writes, referring to women's willingness to conform to male society's expectations of them, 'she had loved something transcending both of them.' Perhaps this was true in the author's life also. (Rodge Glass)

Jelly Roll
Luke Sutherland (1998)
The manner of his prose has been compared to Keith Richards' way with a riff. However, one suspects Luke Sutherland would probably prefer a nod to Charlie Watts, the author's penchant being for the style and swing of jazz over the swagger and savagery of rock'n'roll. Appropriately, having also begun his creative career on the road with the critically fêted (for which read commercially suicidal) Long Fin Killie, Sutherland's literary debut is based on the misadventures of a fictional combo of the contemporary jazz persuasion.

Thinking *Fast Show*, aren't you? Don't. Sutherland's story is anything but nice. For *Jelly Roll* explores race, malevolence and low self-esteem, in the writer's own words: 'searching for existential co-ordinates'. The theme that runs through his career – just three books to date – is that of opposition to the credibility of any definitive notions of race, sexuality, nationality and culture. Pick a confine, a conceit, a construct, and guaranteed Sutherland will seek it out and administer a kick to the yarbles. There's some love in here too, let's be clear, but it tends to be messy, demutualised, unredemptive. Humour and insights, though, there are plenty and Sutherland's musings on music, machismo and the artistic low-life are knowledgeable and never patronising. Vituperative at times, sure, but never patronising.

Queuing up for a beating: Glasgow, bully boys, Pictishness – 'a love of potatoes: staple of the fairyfolk diet' – bigots, druggies, anti-druggies, Anglophobes, Saturday night posers, art school kids, her out of the Cardigans (huh?), and being in a band. Spinal McTap. Without the midgets. Well, in a nation stunted in growth, why

'I am the sword of the Lord, and Famine and Pestilence are my sisters. Woe then to the wicked of this land, for they must fall down dead together.'
James Hogg's The Private Memoirs and Confessions of a Justified Sinner

JK Rowling wrote ten versions of the first chapter of *Harry Potter and the Philosopher's Stone*. She has already written the last chapter of the seventh and final novel in the series, which she keeps in a safe and secret place.

bother? Sample line: 'more alcoholism and cholera teetering pissed in all directions; stunningly beetroot faces glistening, fat red rind and tooth decay, eczema, perms, champagne slacks and white stilettos, gorged leprosy all of it . . . God's zoo . . . Another Celtic bloodbath.' (Rodger Evans)

Jericho Sleep Alone
Chaim Bermant (1964)

Part Bildungsroman, part hymn to the city of Glasgow, *Jericho Sleep Alone* is without a doubt the finest book written about the Scots-Jewish experience. From Bar Mitzvah to an unfulfilling teaching career, Jericho Eli Broch finds himself a perennial outsider and unlucky in love, neither his on-off affair with the flighty Ninna or his financially prudent dalliance with the homely Camilla coming to fruition. Will the sometimes oppressive aid of the Jewish community make all well in his world?

Telling the tale from the awkward pastoral of Jericho's time on kibbutz to his unhappy homecoming with effervescent humour and acute observation, Chaim Icyk Bermant, a Polish Jew and rabbi's son who immigrated to Glasgow at the age of eight, weaves the story of one ethnic minority into the greater tapestry of Scottish life. *Jericho Sleep Alone* is notable not merely for being the first of Bermant's 31 books, or for shining the light on a community not keen to draw attention to itself, but for doing so with such humanising candour, wit and acerbic affection. Despite the old Talmudic saying 'Meshane Hamokom, Meshane Hamazel' (a change of place is a change of fortune), Bermant, who was a member of the Zionist youth group Bnei Akiva in Glasgow, twice left these shores to settle in Israel but returned both times.

While he later left Scotland for the literary lights of London, he never lost his fondness for his adopted homeland, or for its whisky, of which he was an avowed connoisseur. With a further Scottish connection as a screenwriter for STV, and returning to Glasgow for the setting of *The Second Mrs Whitberg* (1976), it was as an irascible columnist for the *Jewish Chronicle*, railing against holocaust museums for their 'pernicious effect on Jewish life', that Bermant became an infamous figure in Anglo-Jewish life. (Dave Martin)

Joseph Knight
James Robertson (2003)

Scots writers often mine the country's tumultuous history to make sense of contemporary concerns. With his bestselling debut novel *The Fanatic*, James Robertson became immediately established as a creator of gripping and innovative historical fiction, cementing this reputation with the rich, compelling *Joseph Knight*, which explored the thorny issue of race, as well as Scotland's guilty complicity in the forging of the British empire.

Following the Battle of Culloden, John Wedderburn is exiled to Jamaica where he thrives, along with countless of his compatriots, as a plantation owner. While abroad, he acquires a slave, Joseph Knight, who he treats as a protégé, bringing the young man back to Scotland with him when he returns, 20 years older, to marry and restore the Wedderburn name to its former glory. Wedderburn has nursed Knight back to health from the near-fatal illness he contracted during the horrific sea journey and, on arriving home, extends an unprecedented benevolence towards the young man. His liberal attitude vanishes, however, when Knight absconds, and Wedderburn spends the next 24 years obsessively tracking who he perceives as his rightful property, a search that takes him from the family pile via the strikingly evoked cityscapes of Dundee and Edinburgh.

The novel jumps back and forward in time throughout, Robertson weaving real-life historical figures and events into his tale (Samuel Johnson and James Boswell make an appearance in one memorably amusing set-piece). The author's skill at effortlessly meshing so many periods, settings and themes (racism, the bond between master and slave, the nature of empire building) is impressive, while the final section, in which the enigmatic Knight finally, passionately voices his determination to live out his days a free man, is especially powerful. (Allan Radcliffe)

King James Bible: The Authorised Version

See panel, page 28.

Lanark

See panel, page 31.

The Lantern Bearers
Ronald Frame (1999)

Until five years ago, had you scanned the Scottish Fiction section of any popular bookseller, chances are your eyes wouldn't have alighted on any work by Ronald Frame. Despite having published 13 books as well as groundbreaking plays and screenplays, the Glasgow-based

Samantha Morton in the 2002 film adaptation

Morvern Callar
Alan Warner (1995)
Reviewer: Bill Duncan

Morvern Callar. 'Morvern': West Highland Peninsula bounded by sea lochs; 'Callar': fresh, attractive. From the black and white cover of my Jonathan Cape first edition, the eponymous heroine stares back at me, her face smeared with peat, initiate of some weird Caledonian land rite, mysterious, unsettling and beautiful. And this first impression took me to the heart of what was special about a novel that has stayed with me for nearly ten years.

1995 was a key date in Scottish fiction: *Trainspotting* was a couple of years old (film/stageplay/soundtrack/ global marketing phenomenon still to kick in) with Rebel Inc and the Chemical Generation in full swing. All very well, but all very Central Belt and all very urban (apart from Duncan McLean) and the authors always seemed to want to talk about football hooliganism, going to raves and taking Es. Some of them even went as far as trying (unconvincingly) to give the impression that these activities meant that they didn't have much time for reading books. And true, there's a lot of deranged partying, drink, music and alcoholic mayhem in *Morvern Callar*. For me, though, the defining quality of the book is its startling lyricism; a near-mystical evocation of its Highland setting through a first-person narrative that shimmers with an ecstatic appreciation of Nature and landscape. This book has more in common with Lewis Grassic Gibbon and Neil Gunn than with Irvine Welsh.

Warner's reconstruction of his native Oban is also a wonderful creation: a crazed zone of anecdotes, myths and improbably named characters. There are fabulous set-pieces: the corpse of Morvern's boyfriend sprawled across his model railway like a giant in a Highland landscape; the Hiphearan drinking whisky out of a salmon; Couris Jean remembering the day on the beach that made her speechless for four years. Many of the sombre late scenes of the novel evoke the dream-like atmosphere of the Highland railway and its surrounding hills and forests at night, drawing on Warner's experience as a railway worker.

All of this is conveyed through Morvern's highly distinctive voice, resolutely Highland in its tone and inflection but contemporary in its field of references to popular culture, individuated through brand names, designer labels, shades of nail varnish, names of bands and favourite tracks. For all of this, I still love *Morvern Callar*; book and character.

Further reading: *The Sopranos* (1998) is about a group of girls in a schools choir competition; *The Man Who Walks* (2002) follows the fortunes of The Nephew, chasing his uncle through the Highlands.

Bill Duncan
is the author of The Smiling School for Calvinists and The Wee Book of Calvin.

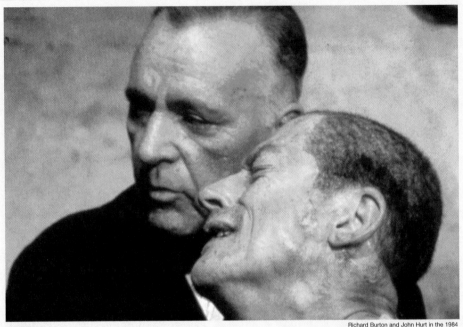

Richard Burton and John Hurt in the 1984
film adaptation, courtesy of BFI

1984
George Orwell (1949)
Reviewer: Denise Mina

George Orwell wrote *1984* on the Isle of Jura, having moved there to escape the sudden, blistering fame that followed the publication of *Animal Farm*. This, somehow, makes it a Scottish book. No more tenuous a claim, I suppose, than lines scribbled on maps by toffs defining a nation. *1984* isn't about a totalitarian future; the title came from reversing two of the digits in 1948 when he wrote it. The book was, and is, about the present and universal dangers inherent in authority. He outlines a society dominated by television screens, the death of privacy, and greasy gin.

The government prohibition on sex seems odd now. Perhaps if Orwell had written it after the sexual revolution the characters would have been subjected to incessant compulsory clumsy sex with a sweaty holiday rep. Winston and Julia would have snuck off to the woods for a bit of celibacy or hand holding. Still, Room 101, now the stuff of parlour games, is a terror as relevant now as then. The concept of tailoring torture by using psychological profiles later became a prototype for the bushtucker trials in *I'm a Celebrity . . .*

Orwell crammed so many elements into the book that every age picks out something else he got right. Of particular relevance now is the social value of a common enemy and governments defending breaches of civil liberties by instilling fear of attack by a foreign enemy. Substitute the rebel leader Goldberg with bin Laden (or

before him Saddam and Gaddafi), and you'd have an analogy bigger than Michael Moore's trousers. Having failed as a literary writer, Orwell turned his hand to social and political comment. He's sometimes looked down on for using cheap tricks (such as interesting the reader or being shocking to get attention), but important stuff can't always be whispered with a small mouth.

When I was young and bad, I stole this book. It was such a good read I stole *Keep the Aspidistra Flying*, too. I can think of no higher accolade. Orwell made me think fiction could be about something other than how awful things are in Hampstead. In *Why I Write*, he said: 'It seems to me nonsense, in a period like our own, to think that one can avoid writing of such subjects.' He's the literary equivalent of the Clash.

Further reading: *Down and Out in Paris and London* (1933) shockingly exposes Orwell's years as a struggling writer; *Animal Farm* (1945) is the world-famous allegorical 'fairy story' attacking Soviet-style communism.

Denise Mina *is the author of five books, including Garnethill, Resolution, and Sanctum. Her new book, The Field of Blood, is published in April 2005.*

PHOTO: RUTH CLARKE

author has never really received the kind of attention accorded to such west coast luminaries as Kelman, Gray or Galloway. One probable reason for this criminal oversight is the fact that Frame's fiction does not conform to any received expectation of what it means to be a Glaswegian author. His characters are mostly middle-class, suburban or rural dwellers; many are not Scottish. Rather, Frame's gift lies in carefully revealing the ugliness that can fester beneath veneers of genteel respectability.

A haunting example of Frame's oeuvre is *The Lantern Bearers*, which won the Saltire Award. The story takes the form of flashbacks related by jaded, middle-aged writer Neil Pritchard, who has been asked to produce a biography of brilliant dead composer Euan Bone. The assignment leads Neil to recall the summer he spent in and around Slezar's Wark, bohemian retreat to Bone and his possessive companion Douglas Maitland. A boy soprano, Neil played muse to the charismatic composer while he constructed his masterpiece, based on Stevenson's essay, the boy's awe gradually turning to hero-worship. When his voice breaks and he is excommunicated, Neil's obsession with Bone leads him at first to stalk clumsily the composer, later – naively or calculatedly, we are never quite sure – contriving to destroy his relationship and career.

The book's brilliance lies partly in this consistent ambiguity about each of the central characters' motivations, but also in Frame's sensitive, wholly believable depiction of the young boy's homosexual awakening in less friendly times.
(Allan Radcliffe)

The Life of Samuel Johnson

See panel, page 32.

The Lighthouse Stevensons
Bella Bathurst (1999)

This is one of the more recent books to make the list, and time will show that it is definitely deserving of its place. In terms of cataloguing Scottish history, few books have better captured a moment and set in stone an incredibly important part of our landscape. Bathurst, through social commentary and sheer detail, has put the history of an oft-overlooked section of our engineering revolution on the map while giving a fascinating insight into Scottish society in the previous three centuries.

Our engineering history is world

renowned and a part of that is both the expertise and innovation brought to the field of lighthouse building. Bathurst brilliantly explains the planning and effort put into placing lighthouses on some of the wildest pieces of rock in the world by a family at the forefront of Scottish engineering. She leads you on fascinating journeys to the four corners of Scotland, bringing to life the raw elements fighting against this family of pioneers. Meanwhile, an engaging history of Scotland's capital unfolds as you learn about the input into Edinburgh by the Stevensons, from the metal-works that still survive in many New Town flats to the creation of a new school to teach the methods of the fledgling industry to a new generation.

All the while, you are continually given great insights into the personalities of the different Stevenson generations, from Robert, who started the tradition of lighthouse building as first engineer to the Northern Lighthouse Trust in 1786, to Alan, who continued the family work until his death in 1971. Robert Louis is mentioned throughout but you are left with the knowledge that while he has become a significant part of Scottish cultural history, his predecessors left a legacy just as crucial.
(Aly Burt)

Lilith
George MacDonald (1895)

George MacDonald has good claim to be the originator of fantasy as a genre with CS Lewis, JRR Tolkien, Philip Pullman and JK Rowling among many others who owe a debt to the Aberdeenshire minister turned fantasist. *Lilith* is the first text to employ the idea of going through a mirror into another world though this other reality is not a neatly allegorical alternative. Moreover, these otherworlds may operate by different rules, as the narrator observes: 'I was lost in a space larger than imagination, for if here two things or any part of them could occupy the same space, why not 20 or 10,000?'

The narrator moves through a succession of surreal landscapes encountering the talking raven, evil wood, white leopardess, house of death and more. Each is vividly clear but imbued with ambiguity. What is the reality status, and the moral or spiritual quality of these events? For MacDonald these questions are always intertwined and in *Lilith* he pushes at the boundaries of literature because he has little interest in conventions or canons. For him, imagination is a doorway to the inner life. CS Lewis struggles to define *Lilith* as

> '"Beyond the Wild Wood comes the Wild World," said the Rat. "And that's something that doesn't matter, either to you or me. I've never been there, and I'm never going, nor you either, if you've got any sense at all."'
>
> *Kenneth Grahame's The Wind in the Willows*

'fantasy that hovers between the allegorical and the mythopoeic', but the effect of reading MacDonald is dreamlike; he is, in the true sense of the word, 'uncanny'.

Lilith is a figure of myth – Adam's first wife and a fulcrum of the narrator's ambiguous journey. Tensions of human/animal, good/evil, body/spirit, and angel/vampire play through the text, finally emerging in a violent conflict. From this, *Lilith* moves onto an openly spiritual plane. As the narrator reflects: 'The darkness knows neither the light nor itself; only the light knows itself and the darkness also.' MacDonald begins the tale with a terse epigram from the Kabala: 'Off Lilith!', and ends it with Novalis: 'Our life is no dream, but it should and perhaps will become one.' (Donald Smith)

Living Nowhere
John Burnside (2003)

Living Nowhere amply confirms John Burnside as one of the greatest writers of prose working today. Born in West Fife, he grew up in Cowdenbeath, before leaving for Corby, an industrial centre in the English Midlands, where his father worked in the steel mills. Expelled from school, he worked variously as a peanut fryer, gasket cutter, gardener and labourer until, working in computer systems design he began writing the poetry for which he is primarily celebrated.

This, his fourth novel, has strong autobiographical elements and tells the coming-of-age story of Francis Cameron, son of a Scottish steelworker growing up in Corby during the 1970s. The strange, violent and dislocated character of this industrial new town is brilliantly evoked, as is the atmosphere of the 1970s, where friendships are cemented by acid, music and a shared alienation. The brutal murder of Francis' best friend Jan precipitates his flight, a journey that cuts him away from his family to search for meaning, belonging and wholeness. The fragmentation of his internal world is evoked in a dialogue between the living and the dead, between love and violence, between home and exile, between belonging and alienation. Burnside's genius enables him to move from the personal to the universal, conjuring the history and feeling of a generation, and speaking directly to an idea of Scotland and Scottish identity that was seriously under siege. 'They wanted to go home,' reflects one character as he thinks of the immigrant Scottish community living in the poisonous shadow of the steel mills, 'but there was no such place as home.'

This is a novel of ideas that dares to demand the reader's attention and thought while remaining accessible. In prose which is beautifully tuned, and exquisitely alive to the nuances of human consciousness, Burnside speaks ultimately of redemption, working that meditative spell that can and should exist between reader and writer. (Marc Lambert)

Madame Doubtfire
Anne Fine (1987)

Three children, a stressed mum, a depressed dad, two hamsters and a quail. It's not happy families. Anne Fine's seminal text on divorce has the lightness of touch and grip of gravity that marks this multi-award winner as one of the finest children's writers of her generation. Daniel Hilliard has moved out of the family home, has his kids over for tea every Tuesday and sees them every other weekend. He's an out of work actor who doesn't deal well with domestic chores; Miranda, his ex-wife, isn't impressed. She can't help being neurotic and he can't stop wanting to kill her in 100 different ways, as he regularly acts out in mime. Lydia, Christopher and Natalie are caught in the crossfire.

Fine evokes the depressing hostility of the atmosphere and its effects on the children with subtle perception: how they all become tense when the phone goes, anticipating a row; how they become silent and withdrawn when their dad makes undermining jokes about mum; how they tolerate miserably their dad's deliberate misunderstanding when they say they want to go 'home'. The dynamics and personalities come vividly into the reader's mind, and while Fine doesn't spare the bitter edges, there's a dry humour too. There's also a lot of love struggling to express itself in better ways and, of course, there's Madame Doubtfire.

The cross-dressing housekeeper who becomes saviour to Miranda and smokes cheroots on the stairs is Daniel in disguise. His ruse to spend time with his family all comes to a high-farce climax when his other job – being a model for the local life class – spectacularly collides with char duty. Fine explores complex emotion and plots a cracking tale that keeps the pages whizzing by, sneaking in wisdom gently. It's no wonder she is so loved by her many devoted fans. (Ruth Hedges)

The Magic Flute
Alan Spence (1990)

For over 25 years, Alan Spence's uncanny talent for cosmically transforming the seemingly everyday in city life has been

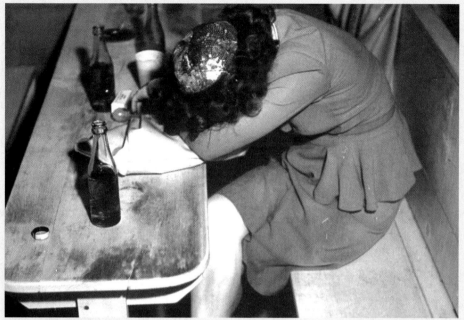

Courtesy of Getty Images

Paradise
AL Kennedy (2004)
Reviewer: Rodge Glass

Alison Kennedy is the kind of writer who gets her contemporaries frothing at the mouth, struggling for ways to describe their admiration. *Paradise* is an excellent example of why, and a bruising, emotional experience. Kennedy is a master of internal monologue, and an expert at knowing where to put the rhythms and pauses in language. Here, she shows exactly what to leave in, what to take out, and how to bring the reader in close to her characters and the moment; a difficult and rare thing in even the best literature.

Many novels have been published about alcoholics, particularly in Scotland, but most have concentrated on men who run from responsibility and distract themselves with filthy thoughts about women they want but know they cannot possibly possess; not the way they would wish, anyway. *Paradise* is different. It takes the reader into the mind of Hannah Luckraft, a lonely nearly 40-year-old who thinks filthy things about sex, is also selfish and frustrating because of her constant and inevitable return to the bottle. But because she is so believably feminine, reading about her is refreshingly different, not simply a retracing of the same drunk male clichés.

There is a plot of sorts, but the story itself is not that important. *Paradise* is simply a book about the vain search for that perfect, still moment when everything makes sense and nothing hurts. Kennedy beautifully describes feelings, like longing for something you want but know you shouldn't have; the need for physical contact above all else; the joy of feeling illicit liquid slip down your throat as you dive into another desperate night of drinking. It seems like whatever Hannah does is the natural thing at that time, as the reader is always made to empathise with her, no matter what. So, though during the book she gets involved with a married man, steals, lies and hurts the people she loves, it all seems perfectly understandable; because life is difficult, and hard to keep under control. And we can all understand that.

'The most reliable measure of a person,' says Hannah early on, 'lies in what they do when they're alone, when they have no need to pretend; are they firm when solitary, or do they slide?' *Paradise* is 343 beautiful, painful pages of being alone with Hannah, watching her slide and slide and slide.

Further reading: *Looking for the Possible Dance* (1993) focuses on a woman's relationships with her father and lover; *Indelible Acts* (2002) examines personal affairs in all their intricate glory.

Rodge Glass' *debut novel, No Fireworks, is published in July 2005.*

Maggie Smith in the 1969 film
adaptation, courtesy of BFI

The Prime of Miss Jean Brodie

Muriel Spark (1961)
Reviewer: Ian Rankin

Jean Brodie is one of the most complex characters in modern literature. As a teacher, she is passionate about her pupils, even if her methods are frowned upon by the authorities. This makes her a rebel, and we should love her for that. But her influence is malign; she attempts to cajole one of her girls into an affair with the art master, as a surrogate for herself, and another of her wards races to her doom in the Spanish Civil War, fighting on Franco's side. Brodie is a great supporter of Hitler and Mussolini, and this is one of her most shocking characteristics.

But *The Prime of Miss Jean Brodie* isn't just about its protean, Jekyll-and-Hyde hero/villain. The schoolgirls are also beautifully drawn, intriguing personalities in their own right, and the book has a complex narrative structure, flowing backwards and forwards in time. Muriel Spark's earliest incarnation was as a poet, and this is very much a poet's work: short and pungent, with no excess fat. An early champion of the 'nouveau roman', Spark was a great admirer of the elliptical novels of Robbe-Grillet. She fuses her knowledge to a very Scottish theme – the twinning of good and evil; the inability of each to exist without the other – and to a lilting east coast style of writing.

If all this makes the book seem worthy and literary, think again. There's a lightness of touch throughout, with an abundance of comic set-pieces. Two of Miss Brodie's 'set', Sandy and Jenny, imagine a series of letters between Miss Brodie and a fictitious lover, one of which ends:

'Allow me, in conclusion, to congratulate you warmly upon your sexual intercourse, as well as your singing.' Such a construction not only makes us laugh, but reminds us that these are impressionable young girls.

Brodie is not in itself a love letter to Spark's native city. There is a tough argument contained at its heart as to the validity of a Scottish education system which, in the 1930s, owed much to Dickens' Gradgrind. Brodie wants her girls to learn about beauty and culture, Giotto and Da Vinci. In effect, what their teacher wants is a fresh batch of mini-Brodies, who can play out in reality the dreams she has harboured throughout her spinsterhood. This heralds her final undoing. It's a book which repays many readings. I was a late convert, having seen the Maggie Smith film first. But it has become a favourite, one of the greatest Scottish books of all time.

Further reading: *The Comforters* (1957) focuses on a woman who is fully aware she is a character in a novel; *The Ballad of Peckham Rye* (1960) charts Dougal Douglas' devilish effects on a factory.

Ian Rankin
is the author of 24 books including The Flood, Black and Blue, and Set in Darkness.

showcased in poetry, drama, short stories and novels. In just three deceptively simple lines in the poem 'ah', Spence perfectly communicates the wonder of watching the stars come out one by one. Meanwhile, his Macallan Prize-winning short story 'Nessun Dorma' exemplifies the Glasgow-born writer's knack for exquisitely juggling manifold themes within a restricted word count, from love and loneliness right through to national identity.

Of his longer fiction, *The Magic Flute* is the most compelling example of Spence's abiding preoccupation with the ways in which characters can be suddenly shocked from their everyday complacency by the realisation that there is something out there (whether that be political, spiritual, cultural) that is way bigger than themselves. The novel tracks the lives of four young Protestant boys growing up in Glasgow during the 1960s and 70s, their warm friendship contrasted with the sectarian bigotry in which they are innocently complicit, enthusiastically marching and playing with the Orange Parade. Of course, Glasgow is a-changing, both physically and culturally, and the four boys who embark on adulthood armed with some big questions are to find their answers in vastly different places. Tam, for instance, breaks for freedom by wholeheartedly embracing the counter culture, New Age spirituality and psychedelic drugs, while Eddie winds up serving in the British army in the north of Ireland.

Throughout, Spence ingeniously interweaves the boys' divergent lives and the events that shape them. Yet despite the period setting, *The Magic Flute* is no nostalgia trip. Typically, the world of Spence's novel is depicted with clear-eyed, unsentimental honesty in the author's characteristic plain, beautiful language. (Allan Radcliffe)

Me and Ma Gal
Des Dillon (1995)
Me and Ma Gal is a novel which continues to defy the odds. Published by a small Scottish press in the mid-90s and republished by a large London firm in 2001, *Me and Ma Gal* twice failed to make Des Dillon as trendy as Irvine Welsh or as fêted by critics as James Kelman. What it became instead was a dearly loved novel among those who read for fun. As Dillon's cheeky-chappie of a book was read and re-read by the kind of people who pay little attention to broadsheet reviews or bestseller charts, its lustre brightened. It should be no surprise, then, that on World Book Day 2003 it was

voted by the public as the novel which best portrayed today's Scotland. It was promptly reissued by its third publisher, but this time awoke, blinking, as a sort of modern classic. It is not hard to see why.

Dillon's book is arguably one of the most frenetic and kinetic, living and breathing of all Scottish novels. Like its lovable narrator, Derek, it just won't sit still. Heeding advice given to him by Edwin Morgan that he should write the way he talks, Dillon lets fly with the kind of tongue wielded in pubs and school playgrounds from Airdrie to Dunoon. But when it's used in the mouth of the freewheeling Derek – the Coatbridge kid with his trusty sidekick Gal on the run from local psycho Septic – it becomes a literary language of its own, rarefied and true. The whole novel crackles with this verbal energy, and nowhere else is childhood friendship evoked with as much vitality as it is here.

Me and Ma Gal is a great Scottish book because, true to the dog-eared spirit of its homeland, it has triumphed over adversity, testament to the power of the way Dillon tells 'em. (Alan Bissett)

Miss Marjoribanks
Margaret Oliphant (1866)
Fittingly for a 'heroine' of Victorian literature, Lucilla, the eponymous Miss Marjoribanks of Margaret Oliphant's novel, is an ingenious sovereign. Her sphere of influence extends only to a section of upper middle-class society in the imaginary English provincial town of Carlingford, but she is both active exponent and victim of the Victorian social order. Oliphant's narrative is driven by Lucilla's confidence and emotional despotism as the young woman sets about revolutionising polite society, meanwhile establishing herself at its hub. Her self-glorification is dressed up as 'public duty', but more interesting is the way Oliphant suggests Lucilla, in her limited, domestic role, provides a mirror image of virtue and decorum which satisfies the vanities of Carlingford's middle-classes.

And while she is single-minded and practical, male characters are conversely governed by their passions. They – as Lucilla refers to her male counterparts – 'do not understand delicate matters of social politics'. Oliphant was famously opposed to women's suffrage but here, as in some of her other novels, the female protagonist has a degree of emancipation. Further, Lucilla's disinterest in marriage, 'until she was nine-and-twenty' is a snub to social convention. These modest assertions of autonomy anticipate the fuller self-realisations of

In 1822, Walter Scott was chosen to organise the visit of George IV to Edinburgh. The King appeared in Highland dress complete with salmon-pink leggings.

female characters in the novels of Virginia Woolf, Catherine Carswell and Willa Muir.

The detached, ironic treatment of these themes is the novel's greatest strength. You're never sure whether Lucilla is really to be pitied, applauded or reproached in the manner of Thackeray's Becky Sharp, for it is indeed the 19th century English tradition to which *Miss Marjoribanks* belongs. Oliphant's family left Scotland when she was only ten, and most of her fiction is set in the south. With almost 100 publications to her name, including over 50 novels, she was Scottish in another aspect: her Protestant work ethic. (Kenny Hodgart)

Morvern Callar

See panel, page 35.

Mr Alfred, MA

George Friel (1972)

Allan Massie once persuasively argued that the idea of a Scottish Renaissance in the 1990s was myopically unfair to writers such as Spark, Jenkins and Linklater, who had produced bodies of extensive work throughout the post-war period. He might have added George Friel's 1972 novel, the quiet masterpiece *Mr Alfred, MA*. The eponymous character is an idealistic, middle-aged bachelor, schoolteacher and failed poet in an increasingly disaffected Glasgow. He sits 'in a common pub with common customers and a common barmaid' and has 'nothing in common with them'. His chaste, but unwise, infatuation with a female pupil, and the rise of gang culture, have a prescient horror as the plot darkens towards an inevitable catastrophe, and a confrontation with the mysterious, malevolent young Tod.

What impresses most about *Mr Alfred, MA* is the linguistic daring through which Friel dissects the tragedy. Mr Alfred's murmured Miltonic quotations rub against the patois of the streets, the crossword puzzles of his frustrated colleagues and the curiously scientific, clinical tone of the narrator. There is a clear debt to Joyce in Friel's prose; particularly in the final catalogue of mania: 'The man's got pedophobia, homichlophobia, dromophobia, xenophobia, ochlophobia, haphephobia,' and on for another 17 diagnoses: 'He's in a very bad way.'

But it is the spirit of the French naturalist writer Emile Zola that seems to brood over the book, as the values of a previous age are eroded by a malign, and specifically urban, modernity. Thirty years before the word 'ned' entered the vocabulary, Friel was already analysing the despair and seething

violence of the inner city which we like to think is contemporary. (Stuart Kelly)

The New Road

Neil Munro (1914)

The image of writers struggling unrecognised in their own lifetime only to be canonised long after their remains have been consigned to paupers' graves is a familiar one. Perhaps we should pity poor Neil Munro (born 1863) whose literary career took the opposite trajectory. Fêted while he lived for his satirical portrayals of Highland life, and serious responses to tumultuous historical events, Munro might justifiably spin in his comfy crypt if he knew the light-hearted *Para Handy Stories* – depicting the adventures of the Vital Spark coaster's idle crew – were his popular legacy.

In fact, Munro's final novel *The New Road* provides the most powerful illustration of the moral complexity and darkness at the heart of the Argyll-born author's best fiction. On one level, the novel is a suspense thriller, being the tale of Aeneus McMaster's attempt to discover the truth about the mysterious death of his Jacobite father Paul. By the end of his journey, our young protagonist has grappled with scheming villain Sandy Duncanson, the steward who has murdered his father and contrived to swindle Aeneus out of his rightful inheritance.

The young man's abrupt passage from innocence to experience is compared to the fate of the Highlands and their folk, currently being dragged kicking and screaming into the 18th century, courtesy of General Wade's 'new road' snaking between Stirling and Inverness. Aeneus, through unhappy experience, has lost patience with the romantic notion of 'noble' Highland chiefs and welcomes progress, while recognising that such civilising measures will sadly hammer the nails in the coffin of the ancient Gaelic way of life. Re-reading *The New Road*, it seems deeply unfair that Munro is often lumped in with the couthiest of romantic Scottish novelists, when much of his work represents historical fiction at its richest. (Allan Radcliffe)

The New Testament in Scots

WL Lorimer (1983)

When the Scots Reformers adopted an English translation of the Bible, a serious blow was dealt to the status of the Scots language which was increasingly banished from the realms of learning and official

James Hogg by Sir John Watson Gordon, The Scottish National Portrait Gallery

The Private Memoirs and Confessions of a Justified Sinner

James Hogg (1824)
Reviewer: Chris Dolan

The Private Memoirs and Confessions of a Justified Sinner is one of cinema's Holy Grails. Plans, scripts, outlines and pitches lie in archives, collections and bottom drawers from Holyrood to Hollywood. Hardly a writer who knows the book – myself included – hasn't tried to adapt it. Written at the beginning of the 19th century, it's screaming out for the big screen. So what's the problem? Nothing in the story itself. Robert Colwan (the original Dorian Gray/Mr Hyde), considers himself above ordinary smelly mortals like you and me. Then he meets a twin more daring and desperate than himself. How much more cinematic can you get?

The difficulty is which *Justified Sinner* do you make? Zone in on the violence and depravity, *American Psycho*-style? Pick up on the dark humour and do a *Witches of Eastwick*? Orson Welles could have used Robert Colwan as Howard Hughes for a case study in madness triggered by loneliness. Scorsese might capture the dull throb of soulless, everyday evil. Tim Burton would invent a satanic Brigadoon peopled by Covenanting bogles and Jacobite brownies. Polanski's your man for doppelganger hysteria. But each of these would give you only a part of the book. James Hogg – his nickname 'Ettrick Shepherd' sums up the myth – is in the great Scottish tradition of untutored, 'natural' geniuses. Perfectly poised between Burns and Stevenson, he was raised on a diet of fairies, ghouls and witches at a time when science and industry were changing the world forever, yet where religious reaction and superstition shackled the masses: a place not unlike today's Midwest. Hogg's is a tale in which reason and unreason meet, where a privileged hierarchy face a disgruntled populace, unsure of their own demands and desires.

Cinematically, it's the devilry and extraordinariness that first appeals. Finally though, it's neither the Great nor Good, the Mad nor Bad, who force the climax, delivering redemption. That's found in the muddle of ordinary characters Colwan encounters. *Justified Sinner* is as much Triumph of the Common Man as Evil Bastard's Midnight Romp. When a Scottish director combining the talents of Alfred Hitchcock, Peter Jackson and Ken Loach comes along, we'll have one hell of a night at the movies. But nothing will ever beat the book. Gruesome, gripping, witty, salacious and candid, Hogg's yarn is not just a Scots classic, it's a universal masterpiece.

Further reading: *The Three Perils of Woman* (1822) powerfully explores the terrible aftermath of Culloden; *A Queer Book* (1832) is a comprehensive collection of Hogg's greatest verse.

Chris Dolan
is the author of Ascension Day and Poor Angels and Other Stories.

Kevin McKidd in the 1994 Wildcat/Citizens production

The Silver Darlings
Neil M Gunn (1941)
Reviewer: Willy Maley

Like Neil Miller Gunn, I'm the seventh of nine children. I know what it means to be caught between the Broons and the Waltons, part Bairn, part John Boy. Growing up, I knew Gunn was a founding figure in the Scottish Renaissance, but the only books of his I read as a boy were *Butcher's Broom* (1934), all doom and gloom, and *The Green Isle of the Great Deep* (1944), which I remembered only for its title. Neither novel suggested that it was fun and games in the Highlands.

By contrast, *The Silver Darlings* conjures up a Golden Age. One moment sticks in my throat like a fishhook. It's at the end of the chapter entitled 'The Wreck', so called because that's how it leaves the reader. Duncan's mother refuses to accept her son has drowned, opening her bodice and placing her boy's bare feet against her breasts till his breath comes back from the beyond. To this day, I carry a card in my breast pocket headed: 'How to Resuscitate'. Who needs the kiss of life when you can be warmed into well-being like that? John McGrath's 1994 stage adaptation reproduced that electrifying episode and captured beautifully the spirited struggle with the sea along a rugged stretch of coastline. In the wake of the Clearances, fishing offered an alternative way of life for the crofting communities displaced by landlords and lambs. The pieces of silver caught in the nets of Finn and the other fishermen are herring, the new currency of

Caithness. Gunn, a fisherman's son from Dunbeath, had his finger on the heartbeat of Highland life and got into Zen Buddhism as he got older, an interest he expounds upon in his autobiography, *The Atom of Delight* (1956).

Some writers display a rampant individualism that would put Thatcher to shame, so it's a joy to read an author with such a strong sense of comradeship and community. Lewis Grassic Gibbon called Gunn 'a brilliant novelist from Scotshire', but *The Silver Darlings* is a heart-stopping story that resonates well beyond these shores. Finn, at the novel's end, sprawls on the knoll at the House of Peace and imagines himself as a white-haired old man: 'Life had come for him.' This is a novel brimful of what Finn's mother calls 'the sweetness of life'. So when the coast is clear, just put your feet up, drink deep, and enjoy it.

Further reading: *Sun Circle* (1930) explores Highland life at the time of the Vikings; *Highland River* (1937) is a nostalgic look at Dunbeam and its strath.

Willy Maley *is Professor of English and Scottish Language and Literature, and convenor of the Creative Writing Masters, at the University of Glasgow.*

culture it had occupied since the Middle Ages. While poetry and song in Scots continued to thrive, the language had to wait until the late years of the 20th century for a monumental work of prose which would give the Word of God a Scots accent.

Lorimer's Scots, which varies to reflect the styles of the *New Testament*'s many authors, takes its energy from both speech and scholarship. A good translation can make a familiar text seem fresh again, invigorating the source as well as the target language. Lorimer's *New Testament* does this with breathtaking regularity. Sometimes verses take on a new pithiness, such as when Jesus tells his disciples that 'ye canna sair God an gowd baith'. Elsewhere, the descriptive power of Scots vocabulary paints biblical characters in bright colours. St Mark's description of John the Baptist gives a sense of Lorimer's exuberant translation: 'John wis cleadit in a raploch coat o caumel's hair an hed a lethern girth about his weyst, an locusts an foggie-bees' hinnie wis aa his fairin'.

Forget a meek and mild Jesus who never breaks into a sweat. In Lorimer's version Jesus speaks with vernacular vigour, exclaiming: 'Hou lang maun I ey thole ye?' to the assembled crowd. Sometimes the result is simply stunning. Consider Lorimer's rendering of the Beatitudes: 'Hou happie the dowff an dowie for they will be comfortit!' From 'Matthew' to 'Revelations', this is a work of verbal energy and poetic beauty which is without doubt one of the greatest achievements in 20th century Scottish writing.
(Niall O'Gallagher)

1984

See panel, page 36.

No Mean City: A Story of the Glasgow Slums

Alexander McArthur and Herbert Kingsley Long (1935)

This cutting edge portrait of working-class life in the worst laid scheme in Scotland sticks out like a sore face. Rarely referred to by its subtitle or complimented for its subtlety, when it was first published Glasgow libraries refused to stock it, while *The Times Literary Supplement* gave it a glowing review: 'Sometimes a "human document" finds its way into print, forcing itself on public attention by the sheer weight of its sincerity, in spite of literary failings. When such a document has artistic value, too, its importance is doubled. Mr Alexander McArthur, an unemployed worker in a Glasgow slum, with the help of

Mr Kingsley Long, a London journalist, has produced such a book in *No Mean City*'.

Despite such highbrow endorsement this jaw-torn tale fell victim to the mean streak of snobbery that disfigures Scotland more than any razor's edge. Dismissed by the small coterie, the book they couldn't bury became a byword for red-raw Clydeside, the nitty-gritty Glasgow of the Gorbals. It deals in dialect and docudrama with a community living on a knife-edge as violence rips it apart. In a world where poverty slices deeper than any flesh wound, it takes more than a sewing machine to make ends meet. Johnnie Stark, the serrated story's young blade, carries out compulsory cosmetic surgery. He's no angel, nor working-class hero, but his brother Peter grasps the nettle of class struggle. How many Scottish novels discuss the great socialist teacher John MacLean? Damn few, and they're all out of print.

McArthur and Long's study of scarcity and scar culture has survived the Glasgow's Miles Better facelift. Its authors sound like a songwriting duo and fittingly, their title lends itself to the theme tune of *Taggart*. Maggie Bell's rasping rendition, more broken bottle than cut glass, captures beautifully the brutal brio of the book.
(Willy Maley)

The No 1 Ladies Detective Agency

Alexander McCall Smith (1998)

Some years ago Mma 'Precious' Ramotswe decided to use her inheritance from her beloved father to open a detective agency in Botswana. Having been met with scepticism by her bank manager ('Can women be detectives?'), she put together her assets (a tiny white van, two desks, two chairs, a telephone, an old typewriter, a teapot and three teacups), hired herself a brainy assistant, Mma Makutsi, and moved into an office shack on land owned by her mechanic gentleman friend Mr JLB Matekoni. And so it was that we were welcomed into the enjoyable world of the Kalahari's Miss Marple.

Writer, academic and bon viveur, Alexander McCall Smith was in fact born in Zimbabwe (called Southern Rhodesia at the time) and educated there and in Scotland. He became a law professor, and it was in this role that he first returned to Africa to work in Botswana, where he helped to set up a new law school at the University of Botswana. Currently a Professor of Medical Law at the University of Edinburgh, he still finds time to work on this superb (and extremely lucrative) series of crime books (the other books include *Tears of the*

'Bounding from my bed, I rushed to the mirror. At the sight that met my eyes, my blood was changed into something exquisitely thin and icy. Yes, I had gone to bed Henry Jekyll, I had awakened Edward Hyde.'
Robert Louis Stevenson's The Strange Case of Dr Jekyll and Mr Hyde

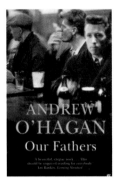

Giraffe, Morality for Beautiful Girls and *The Kalahari Typing School for Men*).

But it was this first book in the series that put McCall Smith on the map, with its fragrant, delicate whiff of redbush tea and malice from the bush. And now he finds himself nearly as sought after for celebrity endorsement in Scotland as Ian Rankin. *The No 1 Ladies' Detective Agency* series has been enthusiastically received throughout the world, and foreign language editions have appeared in numerous countries. (Paul Dale)

One Fine Day in the Middle of the Night
Christopher Brookmyre (1999)

Not just another news-hound turned novelist, Christopher Brookmyre, like the very best who have made the shift from fact to fiction, draws on what's best in journalism: pace, pitch and pressure. His descriptions are concise and his dialogue snappy as he paints a vivid picture of Scotland through a cynical viewing of football, politics and religion; the three at times fermented into a heady home brew. His narratives are directed at an audience unrestricted by regional dialect, even while some characters speak in the broadest of Scots. Brookmyre is an entertainer. And he knows the smack of sensationalism, which he serves in a fleshy narrative with a healthy serving of absurd, obscene and over-the-top violence.

In *One Fine Day in the Middle of the Night*, Brookmyre takes another stab at crime fiction. Like the other novels in his collection it's never short of humour or the divinely bizarre. It is the crackling comedy, as black as an eye that's just said hi to a knuckle, that keeps the pages turning. When Hector McGregor, a soon-to-retire police inspector, is knocked flat out by the fist of a severed arm we can't help but feel the punch and are set deeply under the mercurial control of Brookmyre's farcical thriller.

The cast of characters includes Matt Black, a successful yet highly cynical stand-up comedian. He's travelling to his high school reunion, set to take place on a converted oil rig, hosted by Gavin Hutchison, former student peer and multi-millionaire entrepreneur. But the plan of showing off his floating tourist attraction to old chums may not go as smoothly as planned. Not only does no-one remember him, but his wife has an announcement to make. Meanwhile, a group of mercenaries are harbouring devious plans of their own. (Will Napier)

Open the Door!
Catherine Carswell (1920)

In Alasdair Gray's *Lanark*, Duncan Thaw claims that 'imaginatively, Glasgow exists as a music hall song and a few bad novels. That's all we've given to the world outside. It's all we've given to ourselves.' *Open the Door!*, whose author is probably best known for her 1930 biography of Robert Burns, is one of those novels that Gray's young hero seemed not to have got round to yet. Catherine Carswell's first novel is the story of Joanna Bannerman's attempts to find the freedom denied by her religious upbringing. It is also a fascinating portrayal of genteel society in Glasgow at the beginning of the 20th century, when the fortunes of the Empire's Second City were bound up in colonialism overseas.

Joanna emerges as the most individualistic of her family, the children of Sholto and Juley Bannerman. Her mother is portrayed with great subtlety, saddled by an evangelical zeal wedded to feelings of guilt about having married and she becomes increasingly tormented by Joanna's apparent lack of spirituality. Meanwhile, Joanna struggles to reconcile her bookish, idealised notions of love with the realities she encounters in her relationships with men. As a young woman, she goes to Glasgow's School of Art before marrying and moving to live with her new husband near Florence. Soon widowed, Joanna later moves to London where she defies her mother's conventionality by pursuing a relationship with a married man.

Carswell's portrayal of a journey from girlhood to adulthood is full of nuanced observation; Joanna's love affairs are embarrassing and illicit, unfulfilling and life-changing. *Open the Door!* shows a woman struggling with society's conventions and family expectations, both of which prove unable to meet her aspirations, and finding happiness on the road of her own experiences. (Niall O'Gallagher)

Our Fathers
Andrew O'Hagan (1999)

Our Fathers is about politics, religion, urban regeneration and decay, and identity, both personal and national. More than anything else, however, to me it is a novel about men. Andrew O'Hagan has got inside the psyche of the west of Scotland male and created a story which lays it bare; the anger, violence, repressed emotions, disjointed relationships, unfulfilled dreams but also the sensitivity and love that occasionally creep through in unguarded moments.

Spencer Tracy in the 1941 film adaptation, courtesy of BFI

The Strange Case of Dr Jekyll and Mr Hyde

Robert Louis Stevenson (1886)
Reviewer: AL Kennedy

It's the book everybody thinks they know, but may never have actually read, the iconic Scottish story. One man downs his own slightly unconvincing chemical experiment and becomes two: the good guy and the bad guy. As the bad guy, he wallows in vices and kills; as the good guy, he feels queasy and, having disturbed the Balance of Nature, both guys execute themselves. So now we can all talk about Jekyll and Hyde personalities and mention the long-running Scots theme of the divided self (if not the long-running theme that drinking makes us weird). Plus, we get to see intellectual pride punished and have our morality boiled down into a reassuring Bushworld black and white. God's in His heaven, right next to Calvin and all's viciously Right in the world, yes?

Well, no, because *The Strange Case of Dr Jekyll and Mr Hyde* is much lovelier, more subtly written and complicated than that. Remember that Mrs Stevenson was so determined that hubby should stay a much-loved kiddies' author that she got him to burn the first draft. Remember the story came to him as a nightmare, the fevered vision of a deeply intelligent, passionately moral and complex man. So in Jekyll's foggy, apparently proper Edinburgh – disguised as foggy, apparently proper London – nothing is emptier than a church, the polite facades of enterprising commerce conceal doors into hell and mere chemical interference can unhinge the soul.

Jekyll (RL would have pronounced that 'Jee-kill') is a hypocrite, an outwardly conventional, prosperous man who indulges himself as far as cowardice permits. When he drinks his potion, it will render him absolute; he could become an angel but, lukewarm and weak, he submits to the thrill of evil, the massive energy of unopposed wrong. So Hyde will eventually triumph over Jekyll, as ingenious wrong must, over pretended good.

This is a dark fable from an author who understood physical and moral restraint, temptation and release; whose morality was radical, whose understanding of human frailty was deep and who ended his life as an activist denouncing and opposing the filthy reality behind the cant and pageantry of empire. Read it as a rattling yarn, an atmospheric adventure, but never forget the outrage burning through it, the accusation it quietly levels at a way of life and the question it asks every reader: are you really as good as you think?

Further reading: *Kidnapped* (1886) is RLS' first great critical success, about Jacobite Alan Breck Stewart and lowlander David Balfour's friendship; *Weir of Hermiston* (1896) is the intriguing unfinished tale of a bitterly volatile father-son relationship.

AL Kennedy *is the author of ten books including* Night Geometry *and the* Garscadden Trains, Everything You Need, *and* Paradise.

PHOTO: BRIAN TARR

Vivien Heilbron as Chris Guthrie in the 1971 production, courtesy of BBC

Sunset Song
Lewis Grassic Gibbon (1932)
Reviewer: Ali Smith

I read *Sunset Song* first when I was 16 at Inverness High School. I picked it up grudgingly because it looked like a girls' book, like we were being made to read a soppy classic; it had a line-drawing of a windswept girl on the front which had put me off considerably. I started it resentfully, and became more and more amazed. It was about near where we lived. At that point nothing else was about near where we lived. Chris Guthrie, the main character, wasn't just Scottish, she was actually a Highlander who, astonishingly, liked books. It sounded like nothing else I'd ever read, and at the same time sounded weirdly like the northern-Scottish-English words and syntax we all helplessly spoke. I read way past the place we were supposed to read to for school, and by the end of the next day I'd finished the book.

I've just re-read *Sunset Song*, and its great gripping hybrid of melodrama and realism has left me scorched. There's Chris again: the self split by country and language; the book-lover who's also totally sensual, regardless of both the dark, abusive religion of her father (and forefathers) and the she's-no'-better-than-she-ought-to-be community all round her. And while we're talking about a sense of liberation, Grassic Gibbon's language in the *Quair* freed me to think language could do anything and everything, could be poetic and realist and dark and soaring and local and strange all at once, with sentences longer than breath; but still all about breathing, or how the heart works.

Its real technical (and democratic) achievement is his use of 'you' to mean so many things. It means the protagonist, Chris; it means the communal voice, the local folk voice; it means, and includes, all its readers; it signals an openness in the face of things more usually kept closed: selves, communities, localities. Not that Grassic Gibbon isn't sharp to a too-sentimental reading of his folk-voice: it celebrates the goodness of folk but equally the nastiness and harshness.

Reading *Sunset Song* this time, I was actually thanking goodness for the comic spite at the centre of its communal voice, a relief from the almost untakeable adolescent richness of this first book of three. It goes for the emotional jugular. It has to; this is how lament works. This is the rightful rich ceremony of loss after the war and the end of a kind of innocence.

Further reading: *Cloud Howe* (1933) and *Grey Granite* (1934) are the further installments in the Scots Quair, which take Chris to the cold, hard city of Aberdeen.

Ali Smith *is the author of five books including* Like, Hotel World, *and* The Whole Story and Other Stories. *Her new book,* The Accidental, *is published in May 2005.*

There are three generations in *Our Fathers*. There's Hugh Bawn, a socialist whose great achievement in life had been his role in the post-war rebuilding programme. However, the high-rise blocks that should have stood out as his crowning glory have become a symbol of decay. He is imprisoned and dying on the 18th floor of one of these concrete coffins. His son Robert is an alcoholic whose own life failed to live up to his father's expectations. 'I was never the son my da wanted,' Robert tells his son, Jamie, after Hugh's death. How many Scottish men have said or thought the same?

Jamie arrives back in Ayrshire to visit his dying grandfather, the man who had offered salvation from the destructive nature of the boy's home life. Jamie is also involved in providing housing for the masses, though his vision remains at ground level, unlike Hugh's, which disappeared into the clouds. Hugh's death, inevitable from the beginning of the book, leads to the other two men reconnecting; not in a mawkish or Hollywood-style sentimental way, but in the muttered words and uncomfortable silences of the men in this part of the world. *Our Fathers* was shortlisted for the Booker Prize and is one of the finest, and most honest, Scottish novels of this or any other time. (Paul Cuddihy)

Paradise

See panel, page 39.

The Prime of Miss Jean Brodie

See panel, page 40.

The Private Memoirs and Confessions of a Justified Sinner

See panel page 43.

Psychoraag

Suhayl Saadi (2004)

'Salaam alaikum, sat sri akaal, namaste ji, good evening oan this hoat, hoat summer's night. Fae the peaks ae Kirkintilloch tae the dips ae Cambuslang, fae the invisible mines ae Easterhoose tae the mudflats ae Clydebank, welcome, ivirywan, welcome, Glasgow, welcome, Scotland, tae The Junnune Show.' Suhayl Saadi's debut novel demands attention from its first page onwards, as much by the sounds it conjures as by its story. This is a novel of linguistic fireworks: DJ Zaf addresses his invisible audience in a unique Scots-Urdu patter, with a dash of Gaelic and French thrown in for good measure.

Tonight is the last broadcast of Radio Chandhi, a temporary radio station based in a disused church, and Zaf ignores all requests, choosing instead a very different playlist on his final graveyard shift. He presents the soundtrack of his life, from the Pakistani ballads of his parents' youth to the Asian and Western rock songs of his adolescence. Zaf's memories come as thick and fast as the tracks, and reality and the surreal (Junnune means a trance-like state) dissolve as he recalls the daring escape by his parents from Lahore to Britain, his own destructive entanglement with Zilla who descends into heroin addiction and his relationship with Babs, the blonde nurse who in his mind epitomises whiteness.

This is a story of shifting identity, of hopes and disappointments, passion and separation, and a sense of simmering racial tensions threatening to break into violence on the streets of Glasgow. *Psychoraag* is nothing if not ambitious in its scope: from his radio booth, Zaf's monologue ranges over generations, continents and cultures. At times the sheer energy of the novel becomes almost manic. Saadi has written one of the most original and powerful novels to come out of Scotland for years. (Laura Marney)

Quarry Wood

Nan Shepherd (1928)

Nan Shepherd spent most of her life teaching English in Aberdeen, walking her beloved hills and mountains and encouraging other writers. Yet she will be remembered for the three works of prose fiction she wrote in a five-year burst of creativity in her late 30s. *The Quarry Wood*, *The Weatherhouse* and *A Pass in the Grampians* are all directly informed by Shepherd's experiences. Her debut follows the young life of Martha Ironside, born to a poor family in rural Deeside. Self-possessed and fiercely motivated, Martha keeps the local boys at arms' length, struggles against her circumstance and expectation to go to university, and falls inadvertently in love.

It seems like a small story, but Shepherd's intense prose means it is as much about existence itself as it is about day-to-day life. The language often veers towards melodrama ('spirits' are forever 'flowing') and Martha is a flawed and occasionally foolish protagonist but *The Quarry Wood* works so brilliantly precisely because of these apparent drawbacks. Its conflation of ardent philosophising and blunt everyday speech, rendered in vivid dialect, provides a glorious palette. Martha's spiritualism, meanwhile, contrasts with the drudgery,

Walter Scott's Waverley novels were published anonymously across the world and between 1814 and 1827 creating the first international mass market for books and inspiring paintings, dramatisations and operas.

> 'Glasgow, the sort of industrial city where most people live nowadays but nobody imagines living.'
>
> *Alasdair Gray's Lanark*

sniping and affection of family life and her great aunt's drawn-out death from cancer. Her eventual thawing, with the help of a burbling, illegitimate baby, comes with joy and poignancy.

Throughout, the seasons ebb and flow, gossip twists words in its ill wind and compassion and ambition tussle. Shepherd's love of the land underpins this thoughtful book. It is a connection that many of us, stuck in concrete cityscapes, feel less and less as modernity marches onwards. *The Quarry Wood* works wonderfully as a chronicle of youth, before youth was a marketing tag. But its real power lies in its vivid sense of nature, in all its drabness, colour and dangerous, unpredictable beauty. (James Smart)

Rob Roy
Walter Scott (1818)

The legacy of Walter Scott has done much for tourism in Scotland. Not only does the monument erected in his memory dominate Edinburgh's Princes Street, but his depiction of the Jacobite outlaw Robert MacGregor brought extra recognition to the stunning Trossachs area. MacGregor (more commonly known as Rob Roy or Red Rob) operated in the early 1700s, stealing cattle, looting and selling protection. However, this infamy as a marauder was tempered by the kindness he showed to the poor and disadvantaged, leading Scott to call him 'the Robin Hood of Scotland'.

The novel itself follows Francis Osbaldistone, the son of a wealthy London merchant who is banished from the family home when he spurns a career in the family business in favour of the arts. As he travels to take up residence in his uncle's home in Northumberland, he is both compelled and appalled by the perceived wildness and lawlessness of the northern regions. However, it is not long before he is forced out of the country when a plot by his cousin Rashleigh sends him north of the border to recover his father's money and his own reputation. Once in Scotland, Osbaldistone journeys over a series of borders, from Glasgow into the lowlands, then on to the Highlands themselves. The further north he moves, the more primitive he believes the people to be. However, Rob Roy himself is a rather more complex character, described as an educated Highland gentleman who is also capable of extreme violence.

As the second of Scott's historical 'Waverley' novels, *Rob Roy* plays out the build-up to the Jacobite rebellion and portrays the tension between England and Scotland over the Union. Through the eyes

of a naive Englishman, he gives an outsider's view of the troubled nation, although his portrait of the Highlander outlaw is still strongly romanticised, suggesting sympathy for the Jacobite cause. (Rachael Street)

Sartor Resartus
Thomas Carlyle (1836)

It's always especially interesting to look at texts from a period during which writing was in flux. The years between 1820 and 1840 were tumultuous ones for literature, with a sharp contraction in the production of poetry (caused, in part, by an economic recession) contrasting with a proliferation in new periodical forms and novel publication. Out of this written deluge emerged Carlyle's staggeringly ambitious *Sartor Resartus*, a text only released after a difficult period of negotiation with a number of publishers and journal editors.

The editorial reticence of the time is understandable. Nothing about *Sartor Resartus* is as it seems, and a text based on obfuscation can naturally enervate a reader. It is a false critical biography of a fictional German author, Diogenes Teufelsdröckh, with particular attention paid to his masterwork *Clothes, Their Origin and Influence*. Carlyle may adopt the Romantic method of marrying his overall idea (the reassessment of how we read and write) to a form (false critical biography) that concurs in its complexity and ambiguity, but here, there's nothing as contrived as historically specific methodology. This is writing as apostasy; a reassessment of how we approach literature. The book's narrator struggles to understand Teufelsdröckh's work; we struggle to understand Carlyle's (fictional) critical digestion of it. The evasive nature of meaning in text is thus emphasised.

Sartor Resartus (translated literally as 'the tailor, retailored') is a mind-bendingly, self-reflexive work, written some 130 years before the post-war critics would claim self-reflexivity as a postmodern literary device. Our response to literature, says Carlyle, is as multifarious as life itself, and so why should our criticism attempt to limit a limitless experience? (Johnny Regan)

Scar Culture
Toni Davidson (1999)

A challenging and at times deeply disturbing read, *Scar Culture* is a British *One Flew Over the Cuckoo's Nest* and a dark, twisted spellbinder of a novel. Concentrating on the case studies of three abused children, you become privy to some of the most descriptive and horrifying

To vote for your favourite Scottish book text the word 'VOTE' and the name of the book to 81800

Text charged at your network rate

1995 Citizens production

Swing Hammer Swing!
Jeff Torrington (1992)
Reviewer: Christopher Brookmyre

A confession: it took me what I now regard as a wastefully long time to get around to reading *Swing Hammer Swing!*; wastefully because I would probably have managed to read what became my favourite Scottish novel several more times had I not been so foolishly reluctant. The obstacle was one of expectation, created by the terms in which the book had been recommended – 'it's about a man's house in the Gorbals being demolished'; 'documents the end of an era, the squalor of tenement life and all that'; 'took 30 years to write'; 'immense achievement'; 'ordinary chap, worked in a car factory doncha know' – and thoroughly cemented by its winning a major literary award.

I eventually picked it up out of a sense of Glaswegian civic duty, anticipating a dose of grim urban miserablism that would depress Maxim Gorky. Two pages in, I was swiftly disabused of my misconceptions. Five pages in I was reading through tears. *Swing Hammer Swing!* is the spirit of Glasgow distilled into 400 pages, each tiny drop intoxicating – and thus to be slowly savoured – but you can't help just necking half the bottle at one go.

There is no story – 'plots are for cemeteries' quoth its protagonist – only the meanderings and misadventures of Tam Clay as he awaits the birth of his first child in the final few days before the world he knows is pulled down. I am not going to attempt any kind of summary; suffice it to say this is a book diverse enough to accommodate events such as Tam drunkenly stumbling into a psychopaths' card-school before inadvertently setting fire to the place, alongside Death paying a fruitless visit to the local public toilet, or Shug Wylie's Bum Boutique, to give it its correct title.

No novel has ever encapsulated so much of the language, humour, attitude, philosophy, character and restless energy of the dear green place. I love it passionately, though I still maintain the Whitbread judges gave it the nod for two reasons: one, they didn't get the humour and therefore failed to disqualify it for the literary high crimes of being funny and entertaining; and two, it being the early 90s, they thought the more bizarre passages were actually a Scottish equivalent of Latin American magical realism, rather than merely an accurate depiction of Glasgow on any given Saturday night.

Further reading: *The Devil's Carousel* (1996) is a surreal journey around the interconnected lives of workers in a Glasgow car manufacturing plant.

Christopher Brookmyre *is the author of nine books including One Fine Day in the Middle of the Night, Boiling a Frog, and The Sacred Art of Stealing. His new book, All Fun and Games Until Somebody Loses an Eye, is published in June 2005.*

Robert Donat in the 1935 film adaptation, courtesy of BFI

The 39 Steps

John Buchan (1915)
Reviewer: Brian Hennigan

'He told me some queer things that explained a lot that had puzzled me; things that happened in the Balkan War, how one state suddenly came out on top, why alliances were made and broken, why certain men disappeared, and where the sinews of war came from.' Although written in 1915, this taut, superbly written thriller retains much of its original verve through the sheer perspicacity of the mind that created it. It is far more difficult for a thriller to maintain an ongoing contemporary relevancy than it is for most other genres. Crime fiction can stay true to its period, romance feeds on the broken hearts, not the detail, and chick-lit needs only dummies to buy it, a breed in no danger of dying out.

But for thrillers, particularly geopolitical ones, history changes perspective and the well-informed can come to look ridiculous (Tom Clancy). Not so with *The 39 Steps*. Richard Hannay, a former South African miner, becomes that now clichéd invention: the amateur caught up in a game he doesn't understand. In Hannay's case it's the whys and wherefores of a body in his London apartment and a pre-WW1 German spy plot. As Hannay struggles to retain his freedom and discover the truth, the reader enjoys the type of enjoyable, superbly paced literary yarn for which the word 'rollicking' was devised. Along the way the hero is transformed from establishment figure to pursued rogue, with the security forces coming in for a fair amount of implicit criticism at a time when *Have I Got News For You?* had not yet made such carping so predictably mundane.

While some might, and have, taken issue with the amount of luck that Hannay encounters in his quest, this is to somewhat miss the point: such things do happen. How 'lucky' were the 9/11 hijackers to find a flying school that was willing to teach people who didn't want to learn how to take-off or land? Moreover, the entire brilliant enterprise and architecture of *The 39 Steps* is infused with and underwritten by John Buchan's insider's grasp of what really happens in such worlds.

With a career that included war-time journalism, soldiering, spying and politics, Buchan writes convincingly of the apparatus and methodology of this still largely hidden world. His oeuvre changed the way people thought of thrilling literary fiction (his most obvious successor was Graham Greene) and given the fame of the book through two filmic adaptations, this is as strong a point as any to cross the bridge into Buchan's writing.

Further reading: *The Power-House* (1916) tells of a young lawyer fleeing murderous establishment figures; *Greenmantle* (1916) is akin to *The 39 Steps*, transferred to a German setting.

Brian Hennigan *is the author of Patrick Robertson: A Tale of Adventure. His new book, The Scheme of Things, is published in July 2005.*

PHOTO: LYNDA LAIRD

material on this subject ever written. Seen from the point of view of the victims (in Click and Fright's case) and the abuser (Sad), you are drawn into accounts of sexual and physical attacks which slowly give an understanding of how victims justify this abuse and how the perpetrators balance what they are doing in their own depraved minds. As this part of the novel draws to an end, it's hard to imagine how anything can be worse than what has been doled out so far.

However, the real terror has only just begun. Unresponsive to traditional psychotherapeutic ways, the children are passed on to a special unit set up by two therapists, one of whom just happens to be Dr Curtis Sad, the aforementioned abuser. What follows is a graphic and horrifying depiction of just how wrong pushing the boundaries of science can go.

Adding a new horizon to the landscape of Scottish writing and, in particular, our deep-rooted fascination with crime and horror, Davidson (a teacher in Glasgow) gave Scotland a groundbreaking first novel. Using unusual and highly technical descriptive processes married to an oft-hidden subject area he pushed the boundaries of what is acceptable in writing today and in doing so, put himself forward as one of the most important young voices in literature worldwide. (Aly Burt)

The Sea Road
Margaret Elphinstone (2000)
Historical novels are not easy to get right. If they are under-researched, they don't ring true. If they are over-researched, they groan under a burden of detail that the author was delighted to discover but which may have no place in the story, or was not made new by the imagination. Nor is it enough to get material facts correct; what Edmund White recently called 'brand name history'. Littering the text with period nuggets without going deeper into the culture and mores of an earlier society is as bad as any other anachronism.

The Sea Road, derived from three Norse sagas, largely avoids these pitfalls; Margaret Elphinstone manages to be physically most evocative, while convincing me, at least, that she has worked to imagine how an 11th century Viking might have thought and felt. The novel concerns early Norse journeys to Greenland and then Vinland (that's to say, America). Her principal character is Gudrid, a woman who once sailed with her menfolk to the chilly shores across the Atlantic and who, while in Rome, relates her adventures to a young Icelandic monk.

In one passage, Gudrid, her husband, their longship and crew are trapped in a settlement in Greenland for a terrible, hard winter. As if the freezing conditions aren't enough, a killing sickness strikes them. One by one, the crew die. The hardships are described with chilly power, but Elphinstone also manages the considerable feat of introducing ghosts from which Gudrid must free herself, and does this very believably. Similarly, in the tragic first encounters between the Norsemen (and women) and the natives of North America, she avoids blame and brutality but depicts two warrior societies colliding with predictable results. *The Sea Road* is a short, terse novel, an excellent example of 'less is more'. The prose is often luminous, and the whole a most satisfying read.
(Jonathan Falla)

A Sense of Freedom
Jimmy Boyle (1977)
This is one of the most important books ever published about crime and punishment in Britain. *A Sense of Freedom* is the autobiographical account of how a boy from the Gorbals grew up in the gang culture of the 60s to become 'Scotland's Most Violent Man'; of how, when he was convicted of murder, the prison system tried every tactic fair and foul to break him. It also explores how, eventually, through his art and rehabilitation and thanks to the courage and vision of some officers and politicians, he helped prove the case for prison reform.

There have been many fictional versions of gangland Glasgow, but this is the real thing. Boyle's description of how he took the first steps to becoming the hardman of the streets is riveting and disturbing.

The timing of the story is important. In 1967, Jimmy Boyle was the first high profile figure to be convicted of murder after the death penalty was abolished. Scottish prisons suddenly had to deal with people sentenced to life imprisonment; young men with no hope and no future, who felt that they had nothing to lose, some of whom resolved to take on the system. There followed five years of extreme confrontation with riots, vicious assaults, prolonged solitary confinement, dirty protests, punishment cells, cages and brutality on all sides.

In the end, the system realised it couldn't cope and the Special Unit – an experimental prison inside a prison at Barlinnie – was the result. Boyle's account of when he arrives at the unit and is trusted with a pair of scissors is mesmerising and a moment which

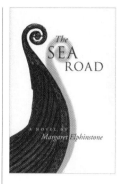

James Hogg and Robert Burns share the same birthday – 25 January.

transformed his life completely. Sadly, the public, the media and too many politicians still have not got the message that prison generally does not work. They should read this book. (Robin Hodge)

The Shipbuilders
George Blake (1935)

Much as shipbuilding was the industry upon which Glasgow was built, so *The Shipbuilders* is one of the twin pillars upon which its literary heritage is constructed. Published in 1935 – the same year as McArthur and Long's *No Mean City* – it gives a humane yet precise image of industrial Glasgow's singular place in 20th century history. Blake, a former journalist, may not have the flash of a Gorbals razor gangster, but he evokes the atmosphere of the terraces as well as he does the big houses of Milngavie.

Leslie Pagan is the wealthy owner of a shipbuilding firm in the final stage of demise and Danny Shields is his former batman during the Great War and one of the hundreds of men he must lay off. Later in his life, Blake said that he pleaded 'guilty to an insufficient knowledge of working-class life and to the adoption of a middle-class attitude to the theme of industrial conflict and despair'. Indeed in scenes when the working man is viewed through the eyes of his excessively loyal patrician boss, he becomes a sentimental cypher of working-class loyalty to his city, country and dead profession which is in direct contrast to the capitalist's own 'desertion, betrayal, surrender'.

Although the book slips occasionally into an industrialised version of the sentimentality he later accused writers of the kailyard school of, Blake, in effect, dramatises his own bias, making his later confession seem harsh; certainly, Shields and Pagan are the most diligent of their respective kinds. His love of the city's scale and its unique history are as much a precedent for Alasdair Gray as his description of the working man's life and his criticism of Scotland's cringing elite are for William McIlvanney and James Kelman. (Tim Abrahams)

The Siege of Trencher's Farm
Gordon M Williams (1969)

The Siege of Trencher's Farm achieved notoriety when it was adapted and released as the nasty, brutish *Straw Dogs* by Sam Peckinpah. The British Board of Film Censors subsequently banned the movie until 2002 because of its graphic violence and a

particularly horrific rape. *The Siege* is a very different beast despite the plot similarities. In Williams' book, as in the film, an American male academic rents a house with his estranged wife in England's West Country and then must defend his homestead from vigilante locals. Peckinpah's film simplifies Williams' more complex plot and argument to a hideous degree.

The academic, Magruder, is writing about Branksheer, an 18th century diarist, a man who was 'at home with Ovid or a London whore, a complete man'. His violent defence of his home is to protect his child and prevent the child molester who falls into his hands from being murdered. An extreme metaphor for the besieged liberal, Peckinpah's hero starts off as an ineffectual mathematician who only becomes a man through bloody deeds. For him, 'a complete man' is the one who kills the most.

Although Williams' book is primarily a deliberation on how traditional masculine values find a place in modern society, it also reflects the differences between American and European liberalism at the end of the 60s. Williams is no Henry James but his writing invests value in a civilisation, something that Peckinpah appears to reject. *The Siege* is also a fascinating watershed between the author's early literary period, as exhibited in his brilliant Booker short-listed examination of Scottish masculinity, *From Scenes Like These*, and *Hazell*, the high paced, testosterone-fuelled detective series he co-wrote with Terry Venables when the latter was still a player at Queen's Park Rangers. (Tim Abrahams)

The Silver Darlings
See panel, page 44.

The Sound of My Voice
Ron Butlin (1987)

After writing favourably reviewed yet largely unnoticed novels and poetry for the best part of three decades, 55-year-old Ron Butlin has the power of Irvine Welsh's popularity muscle to thank for his recently acquired and rightful status as one of Scotland's best kept literary secrets. Asked by the *Village Voice* to write about an unjustly neglected book, Welsh gave *The Sound of My Voice* the kick up the arse it needed to be brought out of obscurity. Republished by Serpent's Tail in 2002, it garnered good reviews and, equally as vital, higher sales. This wasn't before Butlin had gone through more trouble at the hands of the publishing world with his follow-up *Night Visits*, which is rumoured to have sold a pitiful 87 copies on its first release.

To vote for your favourite Scottish book text the word 'VOTE' and the name of the book to 81800

Text charged at your network rate

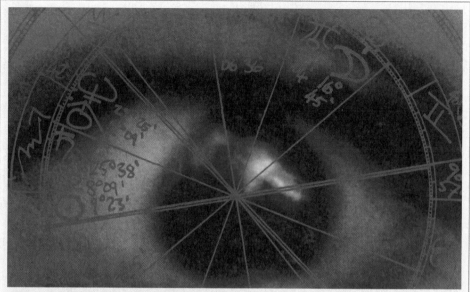

The Trick is to Keep Breathing
Janice Galloway (1989)
Reviewer: Laura Hird

Janice Galloway's debut novel made a considerable impact upon its publication. Winner of the MIND Book of the Year/Allen Lane Award, American Academy EM Forster Award plus a SAC book award, the novel was also shortlisted for the Whitbread First Novel and *Irish Times* International Fiction Prize, placing Galloway alongside Alasdair Gray and Tom Leonard as one of the early exponents of the new wave of experimental, postmodern Scottish writing.

The raw, affecting first-person narrative explores female depression through the eyes of 27-year-old drama teacher Joy Stone, as she tries to find some meaning in life/reason to keep on living following the accidental drowning of her married lover, Michael. Galloway deftly dissects conceptions/misconceptions of bereavement, sanity/insanity, alienation and an ultimate salvation through the reactions of various characters to the death of Michael as Joy struggles desperately to keep afloat, despite the detrimental influence of some glib therapists, worryingly haphazard medication and her uncomprehending friends.

Like Gray's *1982, Janine* and *Lanark*, the novel experiments with typography and form to help illustrate Joy's increasing mental dislocation. Throughout the book, the use of news headlines, disjointed sentences, flashback, speech bubbles, different fonts, floating words and text falling off the page both serve to illustrate her deteriorating mental state and parody the sinister and pervasive effect 'women's' magazines attempt to have in controlling and influencing female behaviour. Perhaps the most effective of these experimental techniques is the mimicking of short script extracts when Joy is communicating with the men in her life – psychiatrists, her boss and ex-boyfriend – as they strive to assert their power over her. What, in the hands of a less accomplished writer, could easily have slipped into a bleak, introspective read is buoyed by Galloway's deft wit and beautifully drawn secondary characters, from the gloriously unhinged Ros who Joy meets in the psychiatric hospital, to her belligerent, bombastic doctor.

The subject matter, confessional nature and dissection of the patient/psychiatrist relationship of the book, led to comparisons to Sylvia Plath's *The Bell Jar* when the book was published but, personally, I feel Galloway's gritty humour, compassion, agonising power of observation, breadth and experimental vivacity struck a far more intimate chord.

Further reading: *Where You Find It* (1996) is a collection of short stories on the theme of love; *Clara* (2002) is an incredibly inventive imagined life of 19th century musician Clara Schumann.

 Laura Hird *is the author of Nail and Other Stories and Born Free. Her new book, Hope and Other Stories, is published in 2006. Check out www.laurahird.com for the best in new Scottish fiction.*

Ewan McGregor in the 1996 film adaptation

Trainspotting
Irvine Welsh (1993)
Reviewer: Louise Welsh

Much imitated but never bettered, Irvine Welsh's *Trainspotting* is my personal numero uno 20th century Scottish book. This novel is now so embedded in Scottish culture that it's hard to remember it's only been around for 11 years. In that time, it's spawned Harry Gibson's excellent stage play, a seminal album that introduced Iggy Pop to a new generation, and a major movie, which helped establish several Scottish movie stars including Ewan McGregor, Kelly Macdonald and Robert Carlyle.

The novel wasn't an obvious candidate for success. Its initial print run of 3000 copies was tiny and its contents were allegedly too offensive for the Booker shortlist. Ignored and unhyped, the book filtered into the mainstream through readers, many of whom – even those whose biggest exposure to drugs was scamming a bit of puff from their big brother's mate – were seeing people they recognised represented in literature for the first time. The whisper started somewhere on Leith Walk and swelled like a George Romero movie crossed with a disaffected Proclaimers video until *Trainspotting*'s popularity and unexpected commercial potential made it impossible for the literary establishment to ignore. The Leith branch of Woolworths began upping its order for jotters as every down-on-their-luck doley and alienated office worker started turning their hand to writing. *Trainspotting* empowered a new generation of Scottish writers, myself included.

The book didn't come out of the blue. The likes of Burroughs and Trocchi had already written about drugs. Leonard, Kelman and others had written in the voices of Scottish working people. But Irvine Welsh built on these existing literary innovations to create a completely original work. He wrote about drug users who didn't have the cushion of a middle-class education and for a generation who had never known apprenticeships, shipyards or slums. Here was the voice of the schemie. *Trainspotting* is now an international phenomenon. It blew me away when I read it back in the 90s and even without the shock of the new, it still stands up as a hilarious, moving, stylish and intelligent novel. The Rebel Inc quote on the cover of my battered paperback copy is no word of a lie: 'the best book ever written by man or woman . . . deserves to sell more copies than the Bible'.

Further reading: *Marabou Stork Nightmares* (1995) is the harrowing tale of haunted football hooligan Roy Strang; *Porno* (2002) returns to the characters from Trainspotting ten years on.

Louise Welsh
is the author of The Cutting Room and Tamburlaine Must Die.

PHOTO: RICH HARDCASTLE

Thankfully, the Butlin renaissance has meant that this book has also reached a wider audience.

Still, why the whole process took so long is a bit of a mystery. Charting the unravelling of a successful biscuit company executive who is barely managing to exist from one drink to the next, Butlin's debut novel is a marvel of restraint. A brilliant and innovative use of second person forces us to empathise with the doomed protagonist Morris Magellan – to almost become him – while simultaneously experiencing unease at our lack of control over what he does.

This mirrors Morris' own experience as he engages in a battle for supremacy over his drinking, his actions and his shame. 'You almost laughed aloud,' Morris says frequently as he convinces himself yet again that he is on top of his life, his game and his colleagues. Laugh a minute, the book is not, yet it's this uncompromising nature and Butlin's unwillingness to have Magellan rescued that makes it so different and so great. (Katy McAulay)

The Strange Case of Dr Jekyll and Mr Hyde
See panel, page 47.

Sunset Song
See panel, page 48.

Swing Hammer Swing!
See panel, page 51.

The 39 Steps
See panel, page 52.

The Trick is to Keep Breathing
See panel, page 55.

To the Lighthouse
Virginia Woolf (1927)
Virginia Woolf is not a name immediately synonymous with Scottish writing. However, her evocation of the Hebrides as a place in which 'the sea is stretched like silk across the bay' should not be denied a position on the list. Conceived at the height of Woolf's affair with Vita Sackville-West, the opening chapters of *To the Lighthouse* stretch across a single day of deliberations about the weather and its suitability for a trip across the bay. In this sense it's a parody of the particular British preoccupation with the weather, seeming to provide the characters with little more motivation than the forecast.

Yet beneath such seemingly banal concerns lie ghosts of Woolf's past – her mother and father as Mr and Mrs Ramsay acting as tools for her strategy of 'writing things out' – and sometimes harsh social comment cushioned in the dunes. Relationship dynamics meander among women who long to give sympathy, support and understanding to the unspoken desires of men who regard them at once with adoration and disdain: 'Women made civilisation impossible with all their *charm*, all their silliness.' Yet though the Ramsays lose their son on the battlefields of World War I, Woolf's novel is no anti-war treatise. Instead, she depicts their quiet despair, set blindingly against the bright Hebridean morning 'as if sails were struck high up in the sky, or the clouds had dropped down into the sea'.

Woolf's writing – though it is often dancing and playful – is not always accessible; her approach to punctuation can give the impression of semicolons and commas being scattered through the text and her choice of words – ardent love as 'helpful', for instance – is sometimes baffling. Yet as the depiction of a place passionately longed for, Woolf's novel resounds with the echoes of the Hebridean landscape. (Katie Gould)

Trainspotting
See panel, page 56.

Trumpet
See panel, page 59.

A Twelvemonth and a Day
Christopher Rush (1985)
A Twelvemonth and a Day is a love song and lament for the vanished 'slow old tuneful times' of life in the fishing villages in the East Neuk of Fife. Rush was born in St Monans, one of the many fishing communities condemned by factory farming methods. He writes of the crews that sailed the Firth; the net-mending and hull-caulking; the manufacture of creels; the whelk-gathering when the fishing failed; the lobsters of August, the herring of winter; practices that Rush clearly thinks preferable to those of the present, when fishing is only 'an industry, a service, a wage packet that used to be a way of life'.

Such halcyon evocations have a long lineage in Scottish writing; there has always been something: fallen leaders, should-have-won battles to bewail and mourn (Rush's most apparent predecessors are Edwin Muir and George Mackay Brown, both of whom wrote Edenic accounts of their Orkney childhoods).

'I'm putting old heads on your young shoulders; all my pupils are the créme de la créme.'
Muriel Spark's The Prime of Miss Jean Brodie

Robert Burns paid for a fitting headstone for Robert Fergusson, after discovering his poet-hero buried in an unmarked pauper's grave in the capital.

Rush's lyricism and reliance on a degree of alliteration more associated with an oral tradition suggests a similar desire to mythicise. But the prose never stoops to sentiment: the moon is 'a drowned skull'; the classroom 'a varnished coffin'.

The book is also a dirge for a time of life: 'that first conscious corner of belonging cut for me out of time'; a youth spent in the fields and on the shore; deciphering the kirkyard graves; listening to eerie tales of things glimpsed at sea. Rush offers a series of portraits of those loved and gone, an attempt to extricate the 'bright splinters of people still sticking in our hearts'. And if the reader sometimes wonders if it was ever really thus and how much its lyric tone can be trusted, then, as Rush says, 'what mattered was the telling'. (Nick Holdstock)

Tunes of Glory
See panel page 60.

Under the Skin
See panel page 63.

A Voyage to Arcturus
David Lindsay (1920)
One of the greatest flights of fantasy in all of fantastic fiction, David Lindsay's debut is not only a metaphorical flight; it's also a quite literal one. Beginning with a séance in Hampstead and a journey to an observatory in north-east Scotland, Lindsay's surreal story blasts its protagonist, Maskull, to the far distant solar system of Arcturus and its lone planet Tormance. There he meets a series of seductive and/or threatening alien beings and finally the world's creator, Crystalman.

This is, of course, allegory. But while it's not difficult to recognise an inquisition into the nature of good and evil and its mirror image of Christian mythology, the meaning of the detailed symbolism remains gloriously (maddeningly, for some) elusive. The enigmatic Maskull may be Jesus or the Antichrist; Crystalman may be God or the Devil; Tormance might be Heaven or Hell. Furthermore, everything has a dual nature: Nightspore, Krag and Muspel are the alternates to the above. Vivid though his prose is, Lindsay refuses to spell out his beguiling vision. If the details of Lindsay's allegorical tale aren't fully discernible, then its origins are less ambiguous. Born and bred a Scottish Calvinist, Lindsay was nevertheless influenced by Nietzsche; such contrary belief systems and thought processes suggest a basis for the book's exploration of morality and philosophy and its inquiry into the meaning of life. The

answers, such as they are, aren't optimistic, which is unsurprising given Lindsay wrote *Arcturus* at the end of the apocalyptic World War I.

Twenty years later, JRR Tolkien did likewise, and acknowledged a debt to Lindsay, whose first book sold only 596 copies and whose writing career never flourished before he was killed by the first bomb dropped during the Blitz. Lindsay's career didn't take off during his lifetime, but his sublime fantasy continues to do so. (Miles Fielder)

The Wasp Factory
Iain Banks (1984)
They say that often an author's debut novel is his or her most autobiographical. Well if that's the case, heaven help Iain Banks. *The Wasp Factory* created a stushie amongst bamboozled literary critics who didn't know how to take this coruscating, visceral attack of a novel, some decrying it as pornographic while words such as 'crass', 'puerile' and 'video nasty' were bandied about elsewhere. In fact, *The Wasp Factory* is an astonishingly accomplished and assured debut, a novel which brought Gothic horror slap bang up to date, which melded the tone of a toe-curling thriller with literary aspirations, unleashing an astounding authorial imagination on the world.

The story revolves around narrator Frank, a 16-year-old misfit in the dysfunctional family from hell. Frank spends his days ritually torturing and killing animals and generally acting obsessive-compulsive as he lives in his strangely warped little world. His mother abandoned him, dad has his own problems and brother Eric has just escaped from a psychiatric hospital where he was sent for setting fire to dogs. Despite all the killing and mutilation that occurs, the book's most chilling aspect is its narrator's matter-of-factness as he goes about his gruesome daily routine. Frank has been kept away from other children and school his whole life, something which lends plausibility to the childish obscenity of his current day-to-day life.

Banks' prose is intense, direct yet dense, packing observations and ideas into every line like there's no tomorrow, yet maintaining accessibility, a blend of inventiveness and popularity that his work has continued to display. Banks has gone on to write even more complex and ambitious books but few have matched *The Wasp Factory* for sheer impact, and the fact this amazing debut hasn't aged a day is testament to its author's timeless talent. (Doug Johnstone)

Trumpet
Jackie Kay (1998)
Reviewer: Alan Bissett

Scotland's writers are a cheeky lot when it comes to sampling. Irvine Welsh and Alan Warner couldn't move for E'd-up *Face* scribes wielding references to acid house. The lilting tones of folk balladry drape the narrative voice of *Sunset Song*. My own debut, *Boyracers*, was as much influenced by the cars and girls epics of Bruce Springsteen as by any book I'd read. Scotland's first foray into the 'Jazz Novel' – a quite formidable canon already containing JD Salinger, F Scott Fitzgerald, Jack Kerouac and Toni Morrison – comes courtesy of Jackie Kay.

Based on the true life story of Billie Tipton, the subject of *Trumpet* is Joss Moody, a jazz musician who, shortly after his death, is discovered to have been a woman. What could have been a one-joke gig or, worse, a routine fictionalised biography, becomes a witty, wiry, cutting, kinetic blast of a book, as emotionally moving as it is formally experimental. A rich cavalcade of perspectives come and go: Moody's grieving widow; their son, simmering with resentment; a scandal-hungry ghost writer; even the confounded coroner who first notices something odd, and whose frantic search for a penis is the novel's biggest laugh.

The effect of this wide range of tones, moods and voices reads like music itself – a shift through scenes that are a kind of blue or a fine romance or strange fruit – until we reach the startling moment which breaks the narrative

right down into a freeform jazz work-out. Kay deftly equates the freedom and fluidity of jazz not only with literary pyrotechnics, but with the instability of the self. This is a book which examines not who we are but, more crucially, what makes us who we are; Kay is equally as ambiguous on identity as a Miles Davis solo is hard to write down. And this is her point: we invent ourselves as we go along. We improvise. We just play. Which is exactly what Jackie Kay does in this book, in precise, beautiful notes.

As a debut Scottish novel, it has few rivals. As a Scottish novel about race and gender it has absolutely no rivals. It is a book of rare charm and confidence, as universal in its message as it is Scottish in its locale. And her poetry is even better. Now that's what I call music.

Further reading: *The Adoption Papers* (1991) explores Kay's experience of being adopted and raised by a white family; *Why Don't You Stop Talking* (2002) is a stunning collection of short stories.

Alan Bissett *is the author of Boyracers. His new book, The Incredible Adam Spark, is published in August 2005.*

Alec Guinness in the 1960 film
adaptation, courtesy of BFI

Tunes of Glory
James Kennaway (1956)
Reviewer: James Robertson

If James Kennaway were still alive he would be 76 and might well be considered the grand old man of Scottish fiction. Like Muriel Spark, though, he would probably live elsewhere: he disliked what he saw as the conformism and 'inbred inferiority complex' of the Scots. 'I suppose if you're going to stay in Scotland and never move out of this teeny little circle and never want criticism from anywhere, then fair enough,' he once remarked. But that was back in 1957. What would he have made of the country in 2005, with its revitalised culture, changed social and economic structure, and its Parliament?

He died in 1968, aged 40, of a heart attack while driving. He had completed seven novels (two published posthumously) and numerous film scripts. Kennaway, according to his biographer Trevor Royle, was 'a classic candidate for a heart attack, somewhat overweight, a smoker with a high voltage lifestyle'. There was an edginess, a liking for risks and emotional if not physical danger, that comes through very clearly in his fiction.

Tunes of Glory, his first novel, grew from his National Service experience in a Highland regiment. The plot centres on the antagonism between Colonel Jock Sinclair, a hard-headed, hard-drinking Scot who has fought his way up from the ranks, and Colonel Basil Barrow, a cold, humourless Old Etonian to whom Sinclair, whose wartime ferocity has turned into peacetime boorishness, seems both offensive and frightening. Barrow arrives to take command of a regimental barracks in a Scottish county town in the middle of winter. He tries to impose his own rules on the mess, is forced into a confrontation with Sinclair, and when things get out of hand cannot take the pressure and commits suicide.

The bare bones of this plot give no indication of the deceptively simple accuracy of Kennaway's prose, nor of his brilliant depiction of characters and indeed an entire society – the male military world enclosed by the high wall of the barracks – in just a few sentences. Kennaway went on to write stylistically and thematically bolder books, like *Some Gorgeous Accident* and his last work, the short but wonderful *Silence*, a love/hate story set in a racially divided, riot-torn American city. But *Tunes of Glory* remains his best-known work, partly because it was made into a superb film starring Alec Guinness and John Mills but also, perhaps, because it is his most Scottish novel. It's an irony, considering his attitude to Scotland, that might have both amused and irritated him.

Further reading: *Some Gorgeous Accident* (1967) deals frankly with infidelity, inspired by Kennaway's wife's affair with John Le Carré; *The Cost of Living Like This* (1969) also focuses on a triangular love affair.

James Robertson *is the author of seven books including* The Ragged Man's Complaint, The Fanatic, *and* Joseph Knight.

The Wealth of Nations
Adam Smith (1776)

Margaret Thatcher, it is said, used to carry a copy of *The Wealth of Nations* in her handbag. It's an apocryphal story but highlights the fact that the deregulation of the 1980s was often undertaken in Adam Smith's name. Yet reading it today, 229 years after it was published, the most striking feature of the book – after its crystal-clear discursive style and moments of dry wit – is the fact that Smith's major work creates a system by which capitalist society can be examined as much as providing a clear hypothesis on the nature of the society itself. The ostensible task of the book, divided into five parts, is to explain why some nations are rich and some aren't but in doing so, Smith has to first create a whole new grammar of political economy.

Among many other things, Smith posits his hugely influential theory of value, describing wages and profit not as rewards but as compensation for the trouble taken in producing or financing a risky strategy. His historically specific remarks, on the other hand, are overlooked. He describes the British defence of the American colonies as pointless and attacks the self-interest of the land-owning classes. *The Wealth of Nations* is debated by every generation of economists because it provides a systematic examination of the economic cycle as a whole.

Yet post-Thatcherite commentators such as Andrew Skinner have criticised previous generations for divorcing Smith's economic system from his moral philosophy. Indeed this approach gets closer to the fundamental dilemma at the heart of Smith's work and of capitalist society in general: how can we be protected from being corrupted by the special interests that are an integral part of our political economy? After *The Wealth of Nations*, Smith attempted to answer this question with a history of jurisprudence but he burned the incomplete work just before he died. (Tim Abrahams)

Whisky Galore!
Compton Mackenzie (1947)

Compton Mackenzie's timeless text is a triumph. Inspired by the real events of 1941, when a cargo ship ran aground in the channel between Eriskay and South Uist, *Whisky Galore!* is the gentle, comical story of how the booty on board became appropriated by a group of Scottish islanders. As the best known of Mackenzie's work, the novel formed the basis for the 1949 Ealing comedy, directed by Alexander Mackendrick.

An innovative text of its time, the book cleverly imagines the dramatic intrusion of the modern world into a small rural Highland community. While the whisky represents the forces of the state and the big business at its core, Mackenzie's wily locals are depicted with charm and imagination, an image far removed from that of the backward, insular Scot. Considering Mackenzie's multifarious background, there's little surprise that such an idea of identity fascinated him.

Born in the late 1800s, Mackenzie studied law but abandoned this career to concentrate on his first play, *The Gentleman in Grey*, and a series of novels. After serving in World War I, he was recruited by MI6, and became director of the Aegean Intelligence Service in Syria. He moved to Scotland in 1928, settling in Barra, the background for this, his most famous comic tale of Scottish life. In 1932, he published the controversial *Greek Memories*, an account of his experiences in the secret services. Before Mackenzie died in 1972, he was calling Edinburgh home, was knighted, founded and edited *The Gramophone* magazine and was president of the Siamese Cat Club. Now there's a CV to raise a wee dram to. (Anna Millar)

The White Bird Passes
Jessie Kesson (1958)

Although Kesson's novel gleans its title from Fiona MacLeod's poem 'The Valley of the White Poppies' (Fiona MacLeod being the pen name of the 19th century writer William Sharp, who is rightly associated with the most sentimentalising and kitsch excesses of the kailyard), *The White Bird Passes* offers a stark and haunting account of the deprivations and poverty of its central character Janie in the 1920s. The novel uses as its raw material Kesson's own childhood hardship, her mother's recourse to prostitution, her unknown father, and her being taken into care in an orphanage. *The White Bird* distils Kesson's compassionate and indomitable siding with the 'ootlin' or outsider in her work, a recurrent recuperation of the voices and perspectives of those outwith communal and societal norms and opinions. The 'home' into which Janie is placed is the antithesis of all that we commonly expect from home – familiarity, belonging, stability – and this sense of a home that is actually the site of profound displacement also typifies a great deal of Scottish writing.

> 'Love makes the world go round? Not at all. Whisky makes it go round twice as fast.'
>
> *Compton Mackenzie's Whisky Galore*

It transpires that Janie's real name is Shona but that her authoritarian grandfather refuses to let her mother or Janie use this due to her illegitimacy and the attendant dishonour. Again this double inheritance, especially the lost or repressed Gaelic genealogy of her own identity, bespeaks a wider Scottish predicament about the self and culture being always at least double if not multiple.

This Gaelic inheritance is also transmitted through folk culture and tradition and it is through the singing of songs and telling of stories with her mother and grandmother that Janie awakens a 'secret self'. Indeed, *The White Bird* is also of enormous importance in anticipating contemporary waves of women's and feminist writing in Scotland for it grants a subversive space shared by these women through which they may articulate their marginalised experiences and concerns. (Aaron Kelly)

The Wind in the Willows
Kenneth Grahame (1908)

As satirical works go, novels exporting the animal instinct have enjoyed a certain longevity, from George Orwell's *Animal Farm* to Pierre Boulle's *Planet of the Apes*. While more upbeat in temperament, Kenneth Grahame's cleverly imagined exposé of late 19th/early 20th century society, *The Wind in the Willows*, is no different. Toad, Mole, Rat and Badger have long left their mark on the Scottish literary scene. At a time when industrialisation was taking a firm hold of Britain's economy, Grahame's *The Wind in the Willows* nicely merged the escapism of a children's book with a timely nod to the social climate of an era.

Grahame's alcoholic father ensured the writer, who was born in Edinburgh in 1859, was largely brought up by his extended family in the west Highlands. After the death of his mother, Grahame was sent to live with his grandmother in the small village of Cookham Dene. This would later become the setting for *The Wind in the Willows*. A banker by trade, Grahame began by writing non-fiction pieces, while dabbling occasionally in the world of fiction. *Dream Days*, published in the late 1890s, showcased Grahame's most famous short story, 'The Reluctant Dragon'.

Written in 1908, *The Wind in the Willows* originally took the form of letters to his young son, Alistair, and were based on talking animals who lived in, and around, a river. Grahame's characters formed the basis of what the novelist felt was missing from society: equality of class, proper distribution of wealth, compassion, generosity and humility. So far removed was the novel from Grahame's previous output that *The Wind in the Willows* was initially ill-received. Later, it would go on to become the author's best known and best loved work. (Anna Millar).

Young Adam
Alexander Trocchi (1954)

Virtually forgotten by his death in 1984, Alexander Trocchi's *Young Adam* was one of the great beneficiaries of Rebel Inc's assault on the Scottish literary canon during the 90s. But it took David Mackenzie's excellent film adaptation, with Ewan McGregor in the lead role, to deliver the long overdue readership and reassessment of this modern masterpiece. Trocchi was a brilliant English and philosophy graduate of Glasgow University, who legend maintains only missed out on a first class degree because he miscalculated his drug intake before the finals. His novel has an existential detachment that recalls Albert Camus; his is a distinctly European perspective that was embraced as part of a Paris literary scene in which he would publish works by Beckett, Ionesco and Sartre. Overshadowed by his reputation as exile, heroin addict and wife-pimp, it's easy to read much of Trocchi's own biography and outsider status into Joe, the novel's insistently subjective, amoral anti-hero.

Travelling on a canal barge between Glasgow and Edinburgh with the owner, his wife and child, they discover the floating corpse of a young woman. As his relationship to the deceased, Cathie, and his part in her death unfold, what startles is Joe's unfeeling detachment, pared back by Trocchi's sparse, gritty prose. Seldom does the shiftless protagonist approach being sympathetic, but unmoored from any recognisable social framework or authority, he possesses a grim charisma and sexual rapacity that dominate the story. Manifesting itself in a series of animalistic couplings with the barge owner's wife and her widowed sister, it reaches its height in the description of a custard assault on Cathie that retains a disturbing ambivalence.

Destined to be deemed a writer who largely wasted his talent, Trocchi was described by Irvine Welsh in double-edged terms as 'the Scottish George Best of the literary world'. *Young Adam* arguably remains Alexander Trocchi's only completely sustained great work. (Jay Richardson)

Courtesy of Canongate Books

Under the Skin

Michel Faber (2000)
Reviewer: Colette Paul

Under the Skin is utterly compelling and thought-provoking from start to finish. It begins with a woman, Isserley, driving through the Highlands on the look-out for male hitchhikers. She doesn't want any weaklings: they've got to be youngish, healthy, preferably strapping, specimens. It's a bizarre opener, made more so by the flat, clean-cut, unremarkable tone of the prose. Isserley's motives are obscured; you don't know if the hitchhiker she picks up is to be treated to a roll in the back seat, or some horrible revenge meted out by a wronged woman.

Finally, after checking the coast is clear, she picks up a man. During the car ride we have access to both characters' thoughts. Isserley worries about what's under the man's clothes – 'Even a starveling could look muscle-bound if he had enough gear on' – and he reflects morosely on his ex-wife, breaking off to have a good eyeful of Isserley's pneumatic breasts. They have some uneasy conversation; the dialogue throughout the novel is authentic in the way that real conversation can be banal and funny and sad all at the same time. After she ascertains that the hitcher has no-one waiting for him, no-one, in fact, who'll care if he disappears, she flicks a 'toggle' that releases a shot of something called icpathua. The man crumples up, unconscious. From this point on you start to feel a sense of horror about what's going to happen next, and this feeling of horror is sustained and added to throughout. Stuff Stephen King; this is a truly frightening read.

I wouldn't want to spoil the plot by saying any more, and indeed one of the great pleasures of *Under the Skin* is the way information is masterfully leaked to you. The revelations are perfectly paced, and you never feel disorientated by them, only urged to read on, faster and faster. Although I don't usually like anything that has a whiff of science fiction about it, this book – like *The Handmaid's Tale* and *1984* – works by incorporating its more fantastical elements into a highly realistic framework and a strong moral message.

As a whole, it presents a humane defence for animal rights, a message that broadens to include compassion for anyone in society who is different. Whatever you take from *Under the Skin*, the characterisation and plot make it so original and distinctive you can't put it down. I know lots of people who've read it and they've all loved it.

Further reading: *Some Rain Must Fall* (1998) is an offbeat collection of short stories; *The Crimson Petal and the White* (2002) is a painstakingly described recreation of Victorian England and the life of a prostitute called Sugar.

Colette Paul
is the author of
Whoever You Choose
to Love.

the Other McCoy

From John Knox to Bill Knox and The Wee Book of Calvin

Although we've styled this section of the next 100 books as the Other McCoy, all the titles listed here are the real deal, from the bleakest side of the Scottish psyche to the brightest lights in new writing. A dark thread runs through Scottish writing, interwoven with a colourful yarn. So here be demons, and here be diamonds. The first book on the list is a blast from the past, and the last is a beauty from the present. From the sexist ravings of a Reformation Rottweiler to the designer Protestantism of Wee Calvin (Calvin Klein), this list shows that while Scotland remains a country given to doom and gloom, it's also one where the vital spark of humour burns bright.

16th–18th Century

The First Blast of the Trumpet Against the Monstrous Regiment of Women
John Knox (1558)
Ever wondered where that vile streak of sexism in Scottish culture comes from? Noxious Knox, Scotland's answer to Bilious Bale, didn't start the fire but he threw some logs on. Straight from the school of hard knocks comes the school of John Knox. His vitriol was directed at Catholic Mary, not Protestant Elizabeth, but that doesn't excuse the hysterical fear of female rule. Burner of books and advocate of universal education, popular pedagogue and merciless dogmatist, Knox remains controversial, to say the least.

De jure Regni apud Scotos, dialogus [A Dialogue on the Law of Kingship Among the Scots]
George Buchanan (1579)
Enshrined in the 'Hall of the Heroes' in the Wallace Monument, Buchanan has his own monument at his birthplace, Killearn. Erected in 1782, the bicentenary of his death, it's a fitting tribute to a towering figure who held professorships at Bordeaux and Paris, tutored James VI, and authored this powerful treatise placing limits on royal power, which massively influenced later generations. In his spare time Buchanan wrote Scotland's history and translated the Psalms into Latin. All in a life's work.

Inquiry into the Origins of Our Ideas of Beauty and Virtue
Francis Hutcheson (1725)
Francis Hutcheson, the kindly father of Scottish philosophy, reacted angrily against the cynicism of Thomas Hobbes, which held that man in a state of nature was nasty, British and short. On the contrary, said Irish-born, Scottish-educated Hutchie, man was cute, Celtic and cuddly. In *Reflections Upon Laughter* and other works, he carefully cultivated generosity and warmth. He argued

for 'the greatest happiness for the greatest numbers', and called for 'calm universal benevolence'. Quite right, too.

An Inquiry into the Human Mind, on the Principles of Common Sense
Thomas Reid (1764)
The son of a Kincardineshire Presbyterian minister, Reid was the founding figure in the Scottish Common Sense School. He served as a Church of Scotland minister himself while establishing a reputation as a serious thinker. The publication of this, Reid's first major work, coincided with his appointment to the prestigious chair of Moral Philosophy at Glasgow University, following in the footsteps of Adam Smith.

An Essay on the History of Civil Society
Adam Ferguson (1767)
Fergie to his friends, adamant to the end, this leading light of the Scottish Enlightenment served as chaplain to the Black Watch, succeeded David Hume as librarian to the Faculty of Advocates, and taught philosophy at Edinburgh. A staunch advocate of active, virtuous citizenship, Ferguson declared that: 'In every commercial state, notwithstanding any pretension to equal rights, the exaltation of a few must depress the many.' It was an attitude that earned him Marx's admiration.

The Man of Feeling
Henry Mackenzie (1771)
When first published, *The Man of Feeling* would bring a tear to a wooden leg, read aloud at weep-ins in drawing-rooms up and down the country. Arguably the finest example of the sentimental novel, it may be worlds removed from the dark thread that runs through Scottish literature from Hogg to Hird, but hey, men should weep.

Lectures on Rhetoric and Belles Lettres
Hugh Blair (1783)
Hugh Blair was preaching the faith in Fife until he started lecturing on literature. Lo! the Chair of Rhetoric and Belles Lettres was created for him at Edinburgh University. His celebrated *Lectures* were published upon his resignation in 1783. Accused of being bland, with a style as engaging as a bucket of warm water, he's praised by admirers as a founding figure in literary criticism.

Outlines of Moral Philosophy
Dugald Stewart (1793)
One of Scotland's towering figures in philosophy, specifically in the Common Sense Scottish School, Dugald Stewart

combined a rigorous intellect with a passionate engagement with psychology. Born in Edinburgh, educated in Glasgow, Stewart succeeded Adam Ferguson to the Chair of Moral Philosophy at the University of Edinburgh. Renowned for his substantial contributions to knowledge, most significantly in *Outlines of Moral Philosophy*, Stewart famously coined the phrase 'Athens of the North' to describe Edinburgh.

19th Century

Marriage
Susan Edmonstone Ferrier (1818)
Susan Ferrier was a writer with the powers of observation of Jane Austen and the eye for the absurd of Tobias Smollett. Walter Scott was an admirer. Ferrier was 15 when her mother died, leaving her to run the household and look after her father until his death in 1829. This, her first novel, is a battle of the sexes in which a cultivated lady elopes with a handsome Highland officer. Published anonymously, it made her name.

Missionary Travels and Researches in South Africa
David Livingstone (1857)
'Dr Livingstone, I presume?' Aye, the Big Bwana from Blantyre, one of the most familiar figures in Scottish history. The original lad o' pairts, one of seven children who combined child labour with studying the classics, Livingstone arrived in South Africa in 1841 as a missionary. His extensive travels took him to the Zambezi region, where he named the Victoria Falls in honour of the British Empress. This is his best-selling account of these explorations.

A Daughter of Heth
William Black (1871)
Born in Glasgow, Black studied at the School of Art, before becoming a journalist and moving to London. He served as a war correspondent in the Austro-Prussian and Franco-Prussian Wars. A popular and prolific writer, Black was a pioneering figure in the field of gothic romance. Most of his works are set in the Highlands, but *A Daughter of Heth*, arguably his most Scottish book in terms of language and theme, is set around Ayrshire.

Johnny Gibb of Gushetneuk
William Alexander (1871)
William Alexander was of Aberdeenshire farming stock, but his days of working the land ended as a young man when a horrific accident led to the loss of a leg. He became a reporter, then editor, with the *Aberdeen Free*

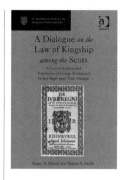

As well as writing horror books, Muriel Gray is a big hillwalker, having written about the joy of bagging Munros.

Press. This first novel started as a serial in that journal, but quickly outgrew its origins and was soon celebrated as a sterling example of Scots vernacular writing.

The Mark of Cain
Andrew Lang (1886)
Anthropologist, biographer, children's writer, editor, historian, poet and scholar, Selkirk-born Andrew Lang was nicknamed 'the divine amateur'. Much of his literary life was spent in London, but he knew Scotland like the back of his hand. An associate of Robert Louis Stevenson and George Douglas Brown, Lang was a renowned classicist who translated the *Odyssey* (1879) and the *Iliad* (1882). *The Mark of Cain* is the work of a mind steeped in history and myth.

Pharais
Fiona MacLeod (AKA William Sharp) (1894)
Paisley-born William Sharp, a twinkling star in the Celtic twilight, attended Glasgow University but never graduated. Obsessed with fairytales and folklore, Sharp wrote plays, poems and biographies under his own name, but found lasting fame under the penname of the fey Fiona MacLeod. *Pharais* is a treasure chest of myths and mysteries. Fiona's true identity only became known after Sharp's death and the divided self of critical Sharp and flighty Fiona is another strange case of Scottish split personality.

The Raiders
Samuel R Crockett (1894)
Crockett's work is often filed under the catch-all category of 'kailyard'. A former Free Church minister, Crockett first found fame through journalism then came to wider public prominence with the publication of *The Raiders*. Set in Galloway, it was an adventure in the tradition of Scott and Stevenson and on the back of this success, he was able to give up preaching and become a writer. 'Kailyard' doesn't do justice to the meatiness of his writing.

1900-1919

The Wee Macgreegor
JJ Bell (1902)
This novel, all too easily dismissed as kailyard kitsch, drew praise from Scotland's greatest living poet. Edwin Morgan called Wee Macgreegor 'an embryo Holden Caulfield in Argyle Street'. Think *Ratcatcher* meets *Scotch'n'Wry* and you're getting warm. Full of the kind of humour and pathos that ages like a good whisky, he's puckish proof that popular doesn't mean puerile.

Gillespie
John MacDougall Hay (1914)
Described by Edwin Morgan as 'anti-kailyard with a rictus', *Gillespie* is a poker-faced story that deliberately sets out to be unsentimental and unsmiling; and succeeds. This nicely nasty novel based around Tarbert charts the rise and fall of self-made man Gillespie Strang. Something's rotten in Argyllshire, and greed and ambition are at the root of it. Gillespie's a big fish, but a cold one. The Devil deserves more sympathy.

The First Hundred Thousand
Ian Hay (1915)
This novel covers the first year of World War I, when nobody knew how or when it would end. Hay fought with the Argyll and Sutherland Highlanders, and the harsh daily life of soldiers feeling the heat in Kitchener's army – gasmasks, grenades and gore – is described in vivid detail. Hay's swift and swaggering style, far removed from the lyricism of Wilfred Owen, paints a not so pretty picture of military life.

On Growth and Form
D'Arcy Thompson (1917)
D'Arcy Thompson's intellect ranged well beyond his chosen field. He was a world-renowned biologist and zoologist, and a prolific polymath who combined classics, mathematics and science. In 1917 he was appointed chair of Natural History at St Andrews University, becoming one of the longest-serving professors of all time. That year also saw the publication of his most famous book, which argues that all animals and plants are best understood in terms of pure mathematics.

South Wind
Norman Douglas (1917)
Anyone described as 'a deplorable character' on his own book jackets has to be good, and Douglas is very good. Famous for pioneering 'Twenties Man' before the decade began, Douglas gives us a memorable character in the shape of Keith, the novel's young redbrick scientist. Likened to Wilde, Douglas thrives on bravura wit. Any novel in which a bishop applauds a woman's action in shoving her cad of a husband off a cliff is wild at heart.

1920s–1930s

The Judge
Rebecca West (1922)
One of several Scottish-Irish authors on this list, West started out in acting, before becoming a journalist. She had a son by HG

ON GROWTH AND FORM
The Complete Revised Edition

D'Arcy Wentworth Thompson

Wells, with whom she had a long relationship. Her first novel, *Return of the Soldier* (1918), dealt with shellshock while *The Judge* is a passionate engagement with the rights and wrongs of women. In 1954 Kenneth Tynan called her 'the best journalist alive'. Her fiction is equally gripping.

The Hustler (Der Puppenjunge)
John Henry Mackay (1926)
A gay Scottish novel published in the 1920s in German by a virtual unknown? Whatever next, men on the moon? Despite a dark pall of prejudice over its sexual politics, Scotland can be proud of its gay and lesbian literary tradition. Set in Berlin, this classic is subtitled 'The Story of a Nameless Love from Friedrichstrasse'. It may seem clichéd now, but it was a pioneering piece of European literature in its day.

Caledonia: Or the Future of the Scots
George Malcolm Thomson (1927)
Anglo-Scottish relations grab the headlines, relegating Irish-Scottish relations to the back pages, but for many the Irish connection is the crucial one. Thomson sees the Scots as 'a dying people' while the Irish – 'a people alien in race, temperament, and religion' – are replacing them. He also believes the 'Scottish lion and the Irish bull will not lie down together'. This disturbing book does for race relations what Attila the Hun did for home improvement. But how far have we moved on?

Dark Star
Lorna Moon (1929)
One of the lesser-known writers of the north-east, Lorna Moon tends to be eclipsed by stellar storytellers such as Gibbon and Gunn. She's not as pronounced in her use of Scots as some of her famous contemporaries. Yet there is a quiet lyrical power and a haunting clarity of expression in Moon's writing, both in her short stories and in this spacious novel which makes her a writer worth lighting on.

Hunger March
Dot Allan (1934)
The days of the demo aren't over, as recent anti-war marches indicated, but the literature of commitment doesn't always please the purist or the privileged. This powerful and purposeful novel responds with imaginative indignation to the poverty and protests of the 1930s. Dealing with a single day when a march ends in George Square and a confrontation with the Glasgow police, its anti-hero, Nimrod, crystallises the contradictions of class conflict.

Scottish Journey
Edwin Muir (1935)
'Muir held up a mirror to the face of Scotland 45 years ago. It is frightening to see so many recognisable features lingering in its glass.' Those are the words of eminent Scottish historian Chris Smout, discussing Muir's *Scottish Journey* in 1979. They still hold true. After an idyllic upbringing in Orkney, Muir moved to Glasgow. His bruising portraits of that city and Edinburgh are beautifully drawn in blood and bile.

Time Will Knit
Fred Urquhart (1938)
Poet Stevie Smith said of Urquhart: 'He does girls very well.' Another critic said he specialised in 'good dialogue and bad women'. In *Time Will Knit*, selected by Book Trust Scotland as one of the 50 Classics of the Century, an all-American kid's Scottish homecoming in 1929 is met with a family history lesson from grandparents who paw at the past like kittens with a ball of wool. Urquhart never drops a stitch.

The Land of the Leal
James Barke (1939)
A real writer with bite, Barke was deeply affected by the political upheavals of the 1930s, including the Spanish Civil War, pouring his politics into his prose. This book follows the Ramsay family from Galloway to Fife and finally Glasgow in search of better times. Poignant in its evocation of a lost childhood in Galloway, it is also fiercely engaged with the pressing struggle between socialism and fascism.

1940s–1950s

Private Angelo
Eric Linklater (1946)
Born in Wales, Eric Linklater spent much of his childhood in Orkney. His major early work was *Juan in America* (1931), a satire on the era of Prohibition. Linklater wrote 23 novels, from biblical adaptations through Viking sagas to Cold War parables. *Private Angelo* is one of his finest works, a comical and compassionate anti-war satire about an Italian peasant who unearths a buried bravery. It's not *Catch-22*, but it'll still hook you.

Fernie Brae
JF Hendry (1947)
Chiefly a poet and short story writer, Hendry took his pint-sized prose and poured it into a barrel. The result is a novel that's a heady brew of images and episodes telling the story of David Macrae, a bright but bereft boy

THE
HUSTLER

The Story of A Nameless
Love from Friedrichstrasse

John Henry Mackay

trying to stay awake in Glasgow during the Snoring Twenties. This town ain't big enough, and America opens its arms to a Glasgow boy with dreams so grand the globe's a village.

Wax Fruit
Guy McCrone (1947)
A big sprawling period piece that's as pleasing to the eye as its title suggests. First published as a trilogy in 1947, the three books brought together as a single volume – *Antimacassar City*, *The Philistines*, and *The Puritans* – wax lyrical on the rise of the Moorhouse family from rural roots in Ayrshire to great wealth and status in Victorian Glasgow, and on to Vienna, jewel in the crown of the Hapsburg Empire.

Dance of the Apprentices
Edward Gaitens (1948)
Another classic of working-class fiction, this coming-of-age story presents an episodic account of life between World War I and the Depression, when a land fit for heroes had housing unfit for habitation. The great themes of the day – pacifism, poverty and socialism – are explored in impassioned prose, as Eddy Macdonnel, a conscientious objector imprisoned for his beliefs, struggles to come to terms with the politics of imperialist and class wars.

Trouble in the Glen
Maurice Walsh (1950)
What is it with Scottish excise men? They take to writing like smugglers take to coves. Originally from Kerry, Walsh befriended fellow excise man Neil Gunn and encouraged him to pursue writing professionally. Walsh's own fame hinged on the bestselling Highland romance, *The Key Above the Door* (1926). A short story by Walsh was filmed as *The Quiet Man* (1952), with John Wayne and Maureen O'Hara, and *Trouble in the Glen* was made in 1954 with Orson Welles, Margaret Lockwood and John Laurie. If you like *Local Hero* you'll love *Trouble in the Glen*.

MacGregor's Gathering
Nigel Tranter (1957)
Nigel Tranter, a prolific writer of children's books, romantic novels and Westerns, was a Glasgow boy enamoured of Scotland around Wallace and Bruce's time. His first foray into historical fiction was *The Queen's Grace* (1953), about Mary Queen of Scots, followed four years later by this book, the first in a trilogy on Rob Roy. Tranter's passionate imaginings of history shaped the perceptions of a wide-reading public.

Dancing in the Streets
Clifford Hanley (1958)
Journalist Cliff Hanley's Glasgow is Old School, worlds removed from Kelman. *Dancing in the Streets* is testament to tenement youth with Dickensian kids scrambling along back court walls, then 'dreep' down. Proverbial shouts ring out: 'Haw, maw throw us down a jeely piece.' Children's chants are recalled with infectious delight: 'If you should see a big fat wummin, standing at the coarnar bummin, that's my mammy.' Purists won't like it, but then, they probably wouldn't be seen dead dancing in the streets.

1960s–1970s

The Desperate Journey
Kathleen Fidler (1964)
This is the story of the Murray family, victims of the Highland Clearances, whose journey takes them from Sutherland to the slums of Glasgow, then on to the Red River Colony in Canada. When the Murray ship comes in it's a familiar vessel called hardship. Cruel landlords, child labour, and poverty: this is the stuff of many a Scottish family history, and here it's a story told with great elegance and energy.

A Green Tree in Gedde
Alan Sharp (1965)
The shipyard worker turned writer is best known now for *Rob Roy*, but fondly remembered for the Peter Fonda vehicle, *The Hired Hand* (1971). Sharp was down to adapt James Hogg's *Confessions of a Justified Sinner*, a project as doomed as its protagonist. *A Green Tree in Gedde* follows four figures in search of themselves, and asks what it means to be 'West Coast Scottish'. Sharp shoots from the lip, rooting through the Wild West legacy of Scottish culture.

The Myrtle and Ivy
Stuart Macgregor (1967)
It's 1958, and young Johnny Ferguson ('the pride of Perthshire'), a medical student at Edinburgh University who is preoccupied with Gaelic lessons and sex education, finds himself savagely torn between Nora and Nell, Ireland and Scotland, Highland and Lowland, country and city. His close Hebridean friend Murdo – 'a Gael first and a Scot second' – resents Lowland Scotland even more than he does England. Johnny somehow straddles these long, deep divisions, but history, religion, geography and sexuality conspire to drive him to a bitter end.

To vote for your favourite Scottish book text the word 'VOTE' and the name of the book to 81800

Text charged at your network rate

A History of the Scottish People 1560-1830

TC Smout (1969)
Any nation's history is divided between mythmakers and academics. Popular and professional historians compete for credibility. This is especially true in Scotland, where historical romance is a hugely important genre: witness the success of *Braveheart* and *Rob Roy*, and the abiding influence of Scott. The gulf between Prebble and Tranter, and the academics who envy their readerships and royalties, was bridged by Chris Smout, the first to combine excellent scholarship with accessible storytelling.

The Tallyman

Bill Knox (1969)
Who pays the tallyman? Bill Knox was a weel-kent face as presenter of STV's *Crime Desk* for 12 years and the reporter-turned-writer racked up 24 novels featuring hard and soft cop duo, Thane and Moss. One asked the questions, the other got the answers. This particular tallyman is a Glasgow loan shark with a taste for blood. When Thane's friend falls victim to the merciless moneylender, the dynamic duo look for a satisfying conclusion in a Highland showdown, where the baddie gets his comeuppance.

The Last Man Alive

AS Neill (1970)
This story of survival began life as a tale told at Summerhill, a pioneering free school Neill founded in 1921, whose ethos was creativity. It opens with a question: who shall bury the dead if only the kids listening are left alive? 'It would take a bit of collecting to get rid of 42 million dead British,' replies Neill, and we're off into a world where anything goes. Meet the fictional millionaire Pyecraft and the real-life Summerhillians.

The Lothian Run

Molly Hunter (1970)
Talent is Not Enough is the title of a collection of essays by Molly Hunter in which she talks about the demands and duties of being a children's writer. Hunter certainly knows what she's talking about, since she's the author of such classics as *The Kelpie's Pearls* (1964), *The Haunted Mountain* (1972), and *The Stronghold* (1974), a Carnegie Medal winner, set on an Orkney island in the Bronze Age. *The Lothian Run* is a book absolutely bristling with ideas that shows she has talent to spare and a technique to die for.

Creating a Scene

Elspeth Davie (1971)
The old adage that those who can, do, while those who can't, teach, applies up to a point in this nimble novella. Foley – art teacher and failed artist – has two young pupils, Nicola and Joe, painting a mural at an old public baths which is being converted into a modern leisure centre. When a local youth mutilates the mural, Joe takes him under his wing. This exquisite story is noteworthy less for its plot than for what it says about painting and people.

Across the Barricades

Joan Lingard (1972)
Three years after the events of *The Twelfth Day of July*, Kevin and Sadie pick up the pieces. Romance blossoms, but the Troubles are tearing the city – and its communities – apart. Barricades go up, bombs go off. Their relationship feels the strain. Will their wedding be marked by the Belfast confetti of falling masonry? The simplistic moral of the story is that the real freedom fighters are the couple fighting to keep their love alive.

My Scotland

George MacBeth (1973)
Written in a surreal style that the author feared had 'no merit', but which 'emerged as the only way to be brief, dense and serious', this was the nearest MacBeth said he would come to writing an autobiography. The aphoristic entries, the poetic titles, the verse interludes and the family photographs all dazzle and delight. This book – pungent, passionate and profound – possesses the immediacy of a diary and the permanence of poetry.

A Truth Lover

John Herdman (1973)
James Hogg haunts many modern Scottish writers, but none more so than John Herdman. Hogg's grim ghost hovers at the edges of this confessional novel in which a young graduate, Duncan Straiton, goes through something of an existential crisis, taking to the highways and byways to exorcise his demons. If you like darkness, duality, Dostoevsky and Dylan then you'll love this. It's a very Scottish story precisely because its brooding brilliance resonates well beyond its borders.

Calum Tod

Norman Malcolm MacDonald (1976)
Born in Thunder Bay in Canada, Norman Malcolm MacDonald returned to Lewis with his family when he was four. Raised on his great-grandfather's croft, MacDonald's first

The movie of Isla Dewar's *Women Talking Dirty* was the first to be produced by Elton John's Rocket Pictures.

A KEVIN AND SADIE NOVEL

acRoss the BaRRicades

JOAN LINGARD

> 'To promote a woman to bear rule, superiority, dominion or empire, above any realm, nation, or city, is repugnant to nature.'
>
> *John Knox's The First Blast of the Trumpet*

language was Gaelic but *Calum Tod* – the tale of a young Gael torn, tongue-tied, tipsy and travel-weary – is written in a haunting and lyrical English. It ends in a blaze of language, the anti-hero burning page by page a book made by 'a mind that was deeply tainted by Southron values'. Brace yourself, it's a beauty.

Devil in the Darkness
Archie Roy (1978)
It's not unusual for scientists to turn storytellers. The smartest science fiction quite often springs from the psyches of those who know how the universe works and can string a sentence together as tightly as an equation. Archie Roy knows full well how the heavens move and what makes time tick. His sci-fi stories are executed with that unerring eye for accuracy one would only expect from an astronomer. *Devil in the Darkness* is a scary trip to the dark side of the mind.

Wild Mountain Thyme
Rosamunde Pilcher (1978)
Born in Cornwall in 1924, Rosamunde Pilcher (née Scott) got her big break writing Mills and Boon romances, notching up ten bodice-ripping yarns under the pen-name of Jane Fraser. *A Secret to Tell* (1955) was her first novel as Rosamunde Pilcher. She made her second home in Scotland and this big breezeblock of a book that would breach the bodices of Brigadoon is set around the small Sutherland town of Dornoch. Will ye go, lassie go? Aye, she'll go.

1980s

Local Hero
David Benedictus (1983)
It's that rare thing: a novel based on a movie. Benedictus adapts Bill Forsyth's massively successful story of Mac, an American businessman with a flashy car (Porsche) and even flashier home (with a sky-line view of Houston) who is sent to Scotland to purchase land for an oil refinery and watch the night sky for comets. The beauty of both the film and book is in the reactions of the locals to this well-heeled outsider.

The Comeback
Alex Cathcart (1986)
This debut novel from a man who worked in the engineering industry tells of Hamish Creese, a joiner in a 1960s Glasgow shipyard forced to make a very sharp exit. Fifteen years later, on a building site Down Under, trouble flares up again so Creese

heads back to his home town in order to lay some ghosts to rest in a Southside pub. Not for the faint of heart, the novel begins with a crucifixion.

Growing up in the Gorbals
Ralph Glasser (1986)
This is the autobiography of a man brought up in the old Gorbals of Glasgow and taken from school at 14 to become a barber's soap-boy and a presser in a garment factory. Against all the odds, and after years of night study, he won a scholarship to Oxford to become a psychologist and economist, concerned with development problems in the Third World. This kicked off his Gorbals trilogy.

Quest for a Kelpie
Frances Mary Hendry (1986)
It's 1745, during Bonnie Prince Charlie's fight to win the British Crown. Culloden is round the corner as we meet Jeannie Main, a tough little fisher lass in Nairn who is warned by a gypsy about a greater future than she could ever expect. This working girl eventually has the fate of two kings in her hands while she maintains an ambition to ride the Kelpie, the great water monster.

A Kist of Sorrows
David Kerr Cameron (1987)
Historical romance is a genre in which Scottish writers excel. Set in Victorian Kilbirnie, among 'the hill crofts and the mud-girt farmtouns' of the north-east Lowlands, the story tells of Morag MacCaskill, a lovelorn lass in the middle of a parish torn asunder by betrayal. Morag's mournful story is bled through the secret journal of Pringle, the Free Kirk minister, and through her own sorrowful kist, a treasure chest for bittersweet memories.

Of Darkness and Light
Barry Graham (1989)
The writer of one of the country's true literary cults, Graham now lives in Tennessee, between a mental hospital, a sewage plant and an American Indian burial ground. Lauded by the likes of Irvine Welsh, his debut (written in a two-month summer frenzy) is a short but blood-chilling tale of psychological horror in the urban wastelands of Glasgow.

Oiney Hoy
Freddy Anderson (1989)
This tale of the wanderings of a 'green fool' toys with Ireland's myths, stereotypes, pretensions and foibles in a gentle but effective satire. It was translated to the

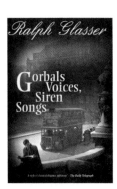

Edinburgh Fringe stage after a premiere in the Great Eastern Hotel, Glasgow and Anderson planned to return to his beloved character but died in 2001.

A Question of Loyalties
Allan Massie (1989)
Etienne de Balafre, half French, half English and raised in South Africa, returns to post-war France to unravel the tangled history of his own father Lucien: was he a patriot who may have served his country as best he could in difficult times, or a treacherous collaborator in the Vichy government? An exploration of the ties between fathers and sons and love and duty, it's also about the anguish of hindsight and the irony of circumstance.

The Shoe
Gordon Legge (1989)
One of the writers in the collection *Children of Albion Rovers*, Legge has often written superbly about friendship, Falkirk and football and this book covers three days in the life of Archie and his pals. Arguments about the beautiful game and the relative merits of his record collection abound. The story presents a culture centred on music, football, sex and the camaraderie of street and pub.

1990s

McX: A Romance of the Dour
Todd McEwen (1990)
'When is life not a story? When it's a joke.' Just one choice line from a book full of them, as we meet our 'hero' McX, his drinking buddy McPint and a Mr McOcalpyse, a bus driver from hell, in a satire about a sodden, grey Scotland full of individuals crippled by booze and Calvinism.

The Other McCoy
Brian McCabe (1990)
It's fitting that Brian McCabe's sparkling novel, characterised by the economy and wit one expects from a consummate writer of poems and short stories, should appear on a list headed 'The Other McCoy'. McCabe is a makar and a multi-tasker, an award-winning poet and short story writer with several collections to his name. He's also a dramatist, mentor, tutor and encourager of others. In fact, he's the Real McCoy.

East is West
Alan Bold (1991)
Alan Bold (biographer, critic, poet, novelist) was a distinctive voice in Scottish letters in the 1970s and 80s. Studies of Byron,

MacDiarmid, Scott, Smollett and Spark, and poetry collections such as the 1985 Scots verse volume *Summoned by Knox*, represent bold efforts to grasp the nettle of a legacy not just living but livid. *East is West* captures the contrariness of a culture open as a field yet closed as a fist.

O Caledonia
Elspeth Barker (1991)
This debut explores the chain of events which, in the social circumstances and mores of 1940s/50s Scotland, cause the bizarre death of a young girl. A dark and lyrical tale of life in the Highlands, it's told by the doomed main character, 16-year-old Janet, who finds solace in reading, learning and nature and generally prefers animals to humans. It won the Winifred Holtby Prize for the best 'regional' novel of the year.

Dead Meat
Philip Kerr (1993)
Dead Meat is an engrossing, bleak thriller about a Moscow policeman weeding out Mafioso elements within the force at a time (of high inflation and massive shortages) when corruption in all sectors is rife. When an anti-Mafia journalist is murdered, all hell breaks loose. Kerr imbues his tough tale with the period's East European imagery: an unsafe nuclear power industry, crumbling infrastructure, corruption and food queues.

The Lights Below
Carl MacDougall (1993)
Having recently brought us the excellent *Writing Scotland* TV series, it may have slipped notice that Carl MacDougall is actually the creator of some fine books himself. In this one, a young man – Andy Peterson – has just been released from prison on a drugs charge of which he is innocent and wants to know why he was framed and by whom. But he finds a very different Glasgow from the one he left behind.

Skinner's Rules
Quintin Jardine (1993)
A vicious killer is stalking Edinburgh's Royal Mile. The discovery of the mutilated and decapitated body of an advocate is followed by the death of his lover, pushed under a train. Detective chief superintendent Robert Skinner eventually learns that the pair had successfully represented the defendants in a rape-murder case. It later emerges that one of the defendants has also been murdered, but complex political considerations prevent Skinner from doing his job properly.

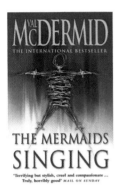

Debatable Land
Candia McWilliam (1994)
This ex-*Vogue* journalist (who previously won a writing competition for the fashion glossy in 1971) won the *Guardian* Fiction Prize with this story set on a sailboat as it travels from Tahiti to New Zealand. Aboard the Ardent Spirit are a painter escaping a failed marriage, the boat's restless owner-skipper and his troubled second wife, two marine nomads and a young woman called Gabriel who captivates the men.

Finding Peggy: A Glasgow Childhood
Meg Henderson (1994)
This classic autobiography of a working-class woman struck a chord in countless homes and hearts. Glasgow girl Meg Henderson grew up in the 1950s and 60s in a big family bruised by the bedlam of Blackhill. Years later, as a journalist, Meg set out to find the truth behind the tragic death of her aunt Peggy. Forget *Angela's Ashes*. Henderson's haunting tale is a tender raking over the coals that'll leave your heart roasted.

Music, in a Foreign Language
Andrew Crumey (1994)
This demanding story of commitment and betrayal deservedly won the Saltire Prize for Best First Novel. The setting is a futuristic Britain in which 'history' is expected to serve the interests of the state and all dissent is ruthlessly and efficiently suppressed. This thoroughly postmodern tale is about dark sexuality, experimental writing, and turns on a mysterious, fatal automobile accident. Add to that mix a deranged pseudo-scientist determined to undermine the reputation of Albert Einstein and you have a brave and innovative gem.

Drivetime
James Meek (1995)
Another writer featured in *Children of Albion Rovers*, the London-born, Dundee-raised Meek has gone on to become a successful journalist, who lived in the former Soviet Union throughout the 90s and reported from Guantanamo Bay in 2004. In this travelogue, Alan wants to start a new life in a new town but he's short of cash for a car to get him there. What follows is a surreal journey across a Europe at war with itself.

The Mermaids Singing
Val McDermid (1995)
In the northern English town of Bradfield four men have been found mutilated and tortured. Fear loves this place, with each living man becoming an island and no-one feeling safe. Clinical psychologist and generally flawed human being Tony Hill is brought in to profile the killer but it appears he might be the next target. This is the book which put Kirkcaldy-born, Manchester-based McDermid on the crime map. Minette Walters is a big fan.

The Orchard on Fire
Shena Mackay (1995)
Shena Mackay was clearly set for big things early on when, aged 16, she won a poetry contest set by the *Daily Mirror*. This was the book which propelled the Edinburgh-born scribe into the big league. It's a 1950s-set tale of a young girl, April, living in a small village in Kent, who attracts the increasing attentions of an older man. *The Orchard on Fire* was shortlisted for the Booker Prize.

The Trickster
Muriel Gray (1995)
Clearly tired of having pitched battles on TV with rock superstars, polymath Muriel Gray chose a new career for herself in horror writing. And so good at it was she that the master of the form, Stephen King, has avowed his support. In this one, a killer is on the loose in the Canadian Rockies and the prime suspect is a chap who has been suffering blackouts and waking up smothered in blood.

The Year's Midnight
Alex Benzie (1995)
In the late 18th century, in the Scottish village of Aberlevin, a man is unjustly hanged. Enraged, the townsfolk vent their anger on the clocktower, quite literally calling a halt to time. A century later, shy, gifted watchmaker William 'Watchie' Leckie is commissioned to repair the now accursed clock. Driven by his growing obsession with the timepiece, Watchie unwittingly unleashes a tidal wave of hypocrisy and hostility that threatens to engulf them all.

Women Talking Dirty
Isla Dewar (1996)
Having a movie, starring the likes of Helena Bonham Carter and Gina McKee, made from your novel is going to do no-one any harm. And sure it was for Isla Dewar with this charming tale of friendship between total opposites Ellen and Cora. Ellen has ended up married to Daniel, but knows something is horribly missing. Cora is outrageous and outspoken but she's keeping some secrets to herself. Still, as long as they have a steady supply of vodka, they'll be just fine.

To vote for your favourite Scottish book text the word 'VOTE' and the name of the book to 81800

Text charged at your network rate

The Warlock of Strathearn
Christopher Whyte (1997)
Retired schoolmaster Archibald MacCaspin decodes an ancient manuscript and finds himself caught up in the story of a child born in the 17th century with astonishing powers: not only can he talk to animals, inflict sores and, conversely, heal savage illnesses, but he also sees dead people. The child's supernatural powers awaken fear and jealousy in his grandmother and a terrible witch-hunt ensues. Whyte's haunting glimpse into the dark side is a feat of true literary magic.

Love and Peace with Melody Paradise
Martin Millar (1998)
A genuine cult character, Glasgow-born, Brixton-based Millar quit his job as a clerk for the local council to become a writer. Often erroneously compared to Irvine Welsh for his literary interest in squatters, raves, drugs and videogames, this (his seventh) novel is set at a free festival, telling the story of a woman who tries to unite a number of disparate groups.

Ascension Day
Chris Dolan (1999)
On a dull March afternoon, three people are seen to rise off the streets of Glasgow into the clouds: a young woman, a bedraggled youth and an older lady who has the modesty to hold her skirts around her knees as she rises. Genuine ascensions or a mere trick of the light? After successful theatre work and short stories, Dolan's powerful first novel lined him up as a major Scottish player.

Pest Maiden
Dilys Rose (1999)
Russell Fairley leads an ordered life as a technician in a blood processing plant. But beneath the mundane surface of his life, all is turmoil. His girlfriend has left him for a trashy American novelist who has even started to put Russell into his books in a less than favourable light and, perhaps worse, a medieval bringer of plagues is lurking. Can our lacklustre hero perform miracles to make life better?

The Stone Canal
Ken MacLeod (1999)
It must be rather hard to muscle in on territory which Iain M Banks has claimed as virtually his own: that of the successful Scottish mainstream sci-fi novel. It's handy then that Banks is a massive fan of MacLeod and little wonder. This hugely ambitious tome has various strands, with one running from the present day in the UK, and another set hundreds of years in the future on New Mars. Each thread revolves around two main characters: they are both political radicals and happen to be in love with the same woman.

21st Century

After You'd Gone
Maggie O'Farrell (2000)
The former *Independent on Sunday* deputy literary editor has lived in each nation of the United Kingdom. In O'Farrell's stirring debut, Alice Raikes takes a train from London to Scotland to visit her family. But when she gets there she witnesses something so shocking that she insists on returning to London toute de suite. A few hours later, Alice is lying in a coma after an accident that may or may not have been a suicide attempt.

A Nation Again
Alison Prince (2000)
As a scriptwriter on *Trumpton* in the 1960s Alison Prince was responsible for the 'Pugh, (Pugh), Barney McGrew, Cuthbert, Dibble, Grubb!' catchphrase. *A Nation Again* is part of the excellent 'Telling Times' series for young people. It's 1700. Scotland's crops fail. Folk starve. Orphan Annie goes to Edinburgh and gets drawn into the debates surrounding the union of Scotland with its English neighbour. A timely tale for post-Devolution Scotland.

Tumulus
Andrew Murray Scott (2000)
'Let it Rip!' and 'Don't Explain!' were the slogans Andrew Murray Scott pinned on his wall while writing this tale of the unearthing of a manuscript which is found to contain a record of the hedonistic life in 1970s Dundee. Archivist Stella Auld goes on an odyssey to track down the author but her attempts are thwarted and her sense of identity and of history begins to crumble from within. The book details bohemian Dundee through the 1960s and 70s to the present day blending fact, myth, pub tales and autobiographical account.

Boyracers
Alan Bissett (2001)
This auspicious debut is about being young, naive and hopeful, amid the pains of living life at hyperspeed in a mad pop-culture world. So, in there we get Stephen King, Pink Floyd, peach schnapps (and lemonade), hope, dreams, Scotland, death-defying driving, *Goodfellas*, Irn-Bru, ten pin bowling, *American Psycho*, car crashes, U2, infinity,

text messages, barmaids, virginity, Radiohead, exams, Tom Cruise, nightclub bouncers and last, but not least, Falkirk High School.

The Dark Ship
Anne MacLeod (2001)
Late in 1918, the Iolaire, a Royal Navy yacht carrying several hundred soldiers home to the Scottish islands of Lewis and Harris, sank in a storm off Stornoway Harbour. Over 240 were drowned, a crushing blow to an island community that had already lost 800 men in the Great War. The tragedy served as the stimulus for this fictional account of friendship and love in the Hebrides.

Exodus
Julie Bertagna (2001)
Exodus is set 100 years in the future. Environmental catastrophes have caused sea levels to rise, and now there are only small isolated pockets of land left. Mara Bell, the main character, lives on an island called Wing, whose area is decreasing each year. She succeeds in gaining access to the 'weave', which appears to be information stored on the internet, and discovers that new cities have been built out of the sea. Can she and her other islanders find a new home?

In the Blue House
Meaghan Delahunt (2001)
Russian exile Leon Trotsky and beautiful Mexican artist Frida Kahlo are two characters in Edinburgh-based Delahunt's impressive debut. The tales and voices of those who history has forgotten also figure in there, such as doctors and engineers in the USSR, Trotsky's bodyguard and assassin, his father, and a one-legged Mexican.

No Great Mischief
Alastair MacLeod (2001)
Alexander MacDonald tells the story of his family from the vantage point of the 1980s. In 1779, driven from his home, Calum MacDonald sets sail from the Highlands for Canada. Reaching 'the land of trees', he settles his extensive family until they become a separate Nova Scotian clan. Assuring one another with their motto: 'My hope is constant in thee', they face up to their many losses.

Not for Glory
Janet Paisley (2001)
Janet Paisley writes not for glory, but gets it anyway. In 1996 her play, *Refuge*, scooped the Peggy Ramsay Award. In 2000 a

"A terrific book. . . fresh, original, smart, devious, and crammed with absorbing lore."
— MARGARET ATWOOD, SUNDAY TIMES

Creative Scotland Award enabled her to write *Not for Glory*, interlinked stories in vibrant Scots, set in Glen Village near her home in Falkirk. Her short film *Long Haul* won a Bafta nomination in 2001, and she was one of ten Scottish finalists in the 2003 World Book Day poll.

The Scottish Nation
Tom Devine (2001)
Post-Devolution, we needed to remember what happened between parliaments. Where had we been all these years? Spanning the three centuries between the Act of Union and the re-establishment of the Scottish Parliament, Devine's book maps out the states of our nation, describing the changes and challenges we've faced. If you don't believe we've had some kind of a revolution over the last three centuries, dip into this scholarly but accessible tome.

White Male Heart
Ruaridh Nicoll (2001)
Dubbed by some as a 21st century *Wasp Factory*, this debut arrived in a raft of publicity, telling the stark tale of Highland buddies Aaron and Hugh. When a young woman – fleeing life in the city and a broken love affair – moves to the area, the ties that bind the boys are slowly stretched to breaking point, leading to cruel violence and horrific destruction. It's grim up north, and gripping too.

Blue Poppies
Jonathan Falla (2002)
In a remote Tibetan village on the Chinese border, Puton, a young woman, crippled and widowed in a terrifying attack, and now seen as an omen of bad luck by the villagers, meets a young Scottish stranger, Jamie. She is scared and he is homesick. As their attraction for one another grows, China invades Tibet. The villagers' epic journey as they flee is a dangerous and harrowing adventure, beautifully told.

Life of Pi
Yann Martel (2002)
Out of the blue, this was the book that won the Booker Prize and put Canongate slap bang on the international map. After the tragic sinking of a cargo ship, one solitary lifeboat remains bobbing on the Pacific. The crew consists of a hyena, a broken-legged zebra, a female orang-utan, a 450-pound Royal Bengal tiger and Pi, a 16-year-old Indian boy. The scene's set for one of the wildest works of literary fiction in recent memory.

Negative Space
Zoë Strachan (2002)
Twenty-four is far too young to die. But that was the fate that befell poor Simon, leaving his grieving sister alone, haunted by the past and terrified of the future, her world blasted open. An unexpected trip to Orkney offers more than just a change of air, and potentially throws up an answer to the tricky question: what do you do when you just don't know what to do? *Negative Space* is a positively spellbinding work from this promising young Glasgow-based writer.

Stone Voices: The Search for Scotland
Neal Ascherson (2002)
Edinburgh-born, Eton-educated Neal Ascherson was described by Eric Hobsbawn, his tutor at Cambridge University, as 'perhaps the most brilliant student I ever had'. Yet Ascherson turned his back on the security of the ivory tower in order to blaze a trail in literary journalism. In *Stone Voices: The Search for Scotland* he returns to his native land. It's a stunning exploration of the sediments of history and identity, in which he combines archaeology, geology and legend to present a thoroughly monumental version of modern Scotland.

Exposure
Michael Mail (2003)
This is a modern exploration of the Holocaust's legacy. Set in London's East End, the novel revolves around a young girl, Suzy, as she embarks on a university course in photography with a first year project on the theme of 'community'. She soon becomes involved with a group of ageing Jewish people, snapping its eccentric members as they go about their various social and religious engagements. But the past becomes a very dark room for her to remain in.

Remembrance
Theresa Breslin (2003)
It's summer 1915 in a small Scottish village where the Great War has begun to alter the course of five young lives. Eighteen-year-old John Malcolm joins the army. His 15-year-old sweetheart Charlotte stays behind to earn her nursing certificate, along with John's twin sister Maggie, who sees the chance to forge a new life for herself. Charlotte's brother Francis sees only tragedy, but still feels the overwhelming pressure to enlist. Alex, who is underage, resolves to reach the front lines.

Scabbit Isle
Tom Pow (2003)
Edinburgh-born Pow was the first Writer in Residence at the Edinburgh International Book Festival. He's the prolific author of poetry collections, radio plays and books for children, and his versatility is potently evident in *Scabbit Isle*. When Sam sees the mysterious Janet, she vanishes into the deserted fields beyond the town. This was once the place to which plague victims were banished. With the assistance of old Mr Carruthers, curator of the local museum, Sam slowly begins to uncover the horror of Janet's story.

The Glass House
Sophie Cooke (2004)
It's easy to see why the opening pages of this novel caught the attention of the judges in a major short story award. People in glass houses shouldn't throw tantrums. Expelled from boarding school, 14-year-old Vanessa watches her autocratic mother unravel. Her friend Alan offers comfort she simply cannot accept. Over the course of four eventful years in the southern Highlands, we hear a moving tale of desire and loss, power and devotion, half-truths and distorted reflections.

No Wonder I Take a Drink
Laura Marney (2004)
Another promising graduate from Glasgow University's creative writing school, Marney produced a witty tale of heavy boozer Trisha, who hasn't been further north than Loch Lomond till she unexpectedly inherits a house in the Highlands. It isn't the cosmic idyll she expected and when she considers joining the Inversnechty Mental Health Awareness Group, Trisha realises things must change. A Highland fling is in order, but everything else is out of order.

The Wee Book of Calvin
Bill Duncan (2004)
The bard of Broughty Ferry exploded onto the literary scene with his quirky short story collection, *The Smiling School for Calvinists*, and roared back with this self-skelp guide. Subtitled 'Air Kissing in the North East', it's a satire on pick'n'mix mysticism and transatlantic psychobabble. At the back of this little gem there's a tongue-in-cheek glossary that includes definitions such as 'bairn – small child, diminutive receptacle of guilt and sin'. You may find yourself laughing your socks off, but don't let that stop you from feeling a little bit ashamed.

> 'What can I do with a girl who has been educated in Scotland?'
> *Susan Edmonstone Ferrier's Marriage*

the Other Three Estates

Poets, playwrights & short story writers

Edwin Morgan

The list of Best Scottish Books in the preceding pages includes some non-fiction, but omits collections of poetry or short stories and drama. Many authors one would expect to find in a list of best Scottish books – from poets of the stature of Burns and Byron to playwrights of the calibre of Barrie and Byrne – are not featured here because their chief works were plays, poems or short fiction.

Readers who want a snapshot or survey of the treasures and truffles in these three forms can feast their eyes on this list. This appendix affords an opportunity to name-check some of those writers excluded from the 200 titles listed in our catalogue of continuous prose writers because they are chiefly antiquarians, diarists, essayists, poets, playwrights, reviewers or short story writers. As well as listing key figures, some recent anthologies are listed in order to guide readers to the best of the latest.

Poetry

Robert Burns would top any list of Scottish writers. The publication of the *Kilmarnock Edition* in 1786 was an event of world historical importance. Burns' comic masterpiece 'Tam o' Shanter' (1790) stands alongside Hugh MacDiarmid's 'A Drunk Man Looks at the Thistle' (1926) as the most memorable long poem in Scots. From Henryson to Fergusson, from Don Juan to Don Paterson, Scotland has been at the forefront of poetry.

Some of Scotland's poets are names to conjure with across the globe: John Barbour, Robert Burns, Lord Byron, Gavin Douglas, Carol Ann Duffy, William Dunbar, Kathleen Jamie, Tom Leonard, Liz Lochhead, Norman MacCaig, Hugh MacDiarmid, Sorley Maclean, Edwin Morgan, Edwin Muir and Don Paterson.

Recent trends in Scottish poetry can be garnered from Donny O'Rourke's brilliant anthology of contemporary poets, *Dream State: The New Scottish Poets* (1994), an invaluable supplement to *The Faber Book of Twentieth-Century Scottish Poetry* (1992), edited by Douglas Dunn. The popular tradition has been celebrated in Tom Leonard's *Radical Renfrew* (1990).

Drama

Scottish theatre has strutted its stuff on the world's stage for centuries, but only in the last year has it had a National Theatre to call its own. Appropriately enough, it's an idea rather than a space. David Lindsay's *A Satire of the Three Estates* (1520) is a cornerstone. Since the 16th century, Scottish playwrights have been pioneers, blazing a trail from page to stage. Some names to conjure with are JM Barrie, James Bridie, Gregory Burke, John Byrne, Joe Corrie, Sue Glover, David Harrower, John Home, David Lindsay, Liz Lochhead, John McGrath and Ena Lamont Stewart.

A dozen very Scottish plays that would grace any nation's stage are David Lindsay's *A Satire of the Three Estates* (1520); John Home's *Douglas* (1756); JM Barrie's *Peter Pan* (1904); Joe Corrie's *In Time o' Strife* (1927); James Bridie's *The Anatomist* (1930); Ena Lamont Stewart's *Men Should Weep* (1946); John McGrath's *The Cheviot, the Stag, and the Black, Black Oil* (1973); John Byrne's *The Slab Boys* (1978); Liz Lochhead's *Mary Queen of Scots Got Her Head Chopped Off* (1987); Sue Glover's *Bondagers* (1993); David Harrower's *Knives in Hens* (1997); and Gregory Burke's *Gagarin Way* (2001).

Recent work in Scottish theatre can be found in excellent anthologies like *Scot-Free: New Scottish Plays* (1990), edited by Alasdair Cameron; *Twentieth-Century Scottish Drama: An Anthology* (2001), edited by Cairns Craig and Randall Stevenson; *Scots Plays of the Seventies* (2001), edited by Bill Findlay; *Scotland Plays: New Scottish Drama* (1998), edited by Philip Howard; and *Made in Scotland: An Anthology of New Scottish Plays* (1995), edited by Ian Brown and Mark Fisher.

Short Stories

Good whisky comes in small glasses, and Scotland excels in the short story form. Most of our major writers have drunk deep at the font of the short story, and gone back for more: John Burnside, Anne Donovan, Janice Galloway, Alasdair Gray, James Kelman, Alison Kennedy and Irvine Welsh are all experts in the form. Carl MacDougall's wonderful anthology, *The Devil and the Giro: Two Centuries of Scottish Stories* (1991), is testament to the quality and craft displayed by our writers of short fiction. *The Oxford Book of Scottish Short Stories* (1995), edited by Douglas Dunn, is further proof of the skill and daring of Scottish writers. Other anthologies that will whet the appetite include *Scottish Love Stories* (1995),

edited by Susie Maguire and Marion Sinclair; *Ahead of its Time: A Clocktower Press Anthology* (1997), edited by Duncan McLean; *Children of Albion Rovers* (1997), edited by Kevin Williamson; *Something Wicked: Scottish Crime Fiction* (1999), edited by Susie Maguire and Amanda Hargreaves; and *The Vintage Book of Contemporary Scottish Fiction* (1999), edited by Peter Kravitz.

Gay and lesbian writing has taken pride of place in the new Scotland. Its late flowering has been one of the signs of a nation coming of age, and some of its success stories deserve special mention. Recent anthologies include *And Thus Will I Freely Sing* (1989), edited by Toni Davidson; *The Crazy Jig* (1992), edited by Joanne Winning; *Footsteps and Witnesses* (1993), edited by Bob Cant; and *Borderline: The Mainstream Book of Scottish Gay Writing* (2001), edited by Joseph Mills. The Glasgay! Festival was launched in the early 1990s, supplanting Mayfest as the place to be seen and heard, and confirming the relationship between print and public performance in establishing a diverse culture.

The Slab Boys

Although Burns casts a giant shadow over all his successors, there is one writer who looms large in the present, and I would like to dedicate this list to Scotland's poet laureate, Edwin Morgan. Last year the Scottish Executive appointed him 'Scots Makar', a fitting title for a writer who combines the best of the old and the new. If the *Kilmarnock Edition* is the book with which Burns put Scotland on the map, then Edwin Morgan's *Sonnets from Scotland* (1984) will keep it there forever.

Morgan, more than anyone, represents Scottish writing at its most vital and vivid. His poems, plays, essays and translations have brought us into the 21st century. Professor Morgan is no stranger to lists. In 1987, he produced for Book Trust Scotland and the British Council a Scottish companion to Margaret Drabble's *Twentieth Century Classics* (1986). Morgan's work was entitled *Twentieth Century Scottish Classics*, and it was a characteristically subtle enterprise, bold in its choices and inclusive in its coverage.

This present list – including this appendix – enters into the spirit of Morgan's heady mix of old spice and new books on the block. It covers all of God's green acres, most of the Devil's domain, and all stops in between.
Professor Willy Maley

Irvine Welsh

index

of authors and books

For poets, playwrights and short story writers see The Other Three Estates pages 76 & 77.